Lord of Legends is a blockbuster book. Eve., ..., every paragraph, every chapter is as action-packed as a movie trailer. My longtime friend helps readers see how comic books, films, and even the classics all point to Jesus—the epic hero of the story we're all living. Everyone from teen fans of the MCU to pastors attempting *Lord of the Rings* references in their sermons will benefit from this book. Pastor Eric Eichinger is the Obi-Wan Kenobi we need to understand our own place in Christ's story.

REV. DR. BENJAMIN D. HAUPT, ASSOCIATE PROVOST, ASSOCIATE PROFESSOR
OF PRACTICAL THEOLOGY, CONCORDIA SEMINARY, ST. LOUIS, MO

Lord of Legends connects, compares, and contrasts the true story of Scripture with many well-known adventure stories, ancient and modern, that our world likes to tell. Eichinger has challenged me, a father of boys, to put to godly use my knowledge of epic sagas, lightsabers, and superheroes. He has also motivated me to hone my pastoral storytelling skills when speaking of the greatest Hero, Jesus. Whether a parent, pastor, or some other person, this book will strengthen your faith and prepare you with the Word, that you may help any fan of legends to meet the true Lord.

REV. JONATHAN GRUEN, SENIOR PASTOR,
BEAUTIFUL SAVIOR LUTHERAN CHURCH, LEE'S SUMMIT, MO

Lord of Legends is a fantastic effort at sharing Christ in today's world. It is well researched, creative, and should resonate easily with our current culture. Eric exhibits a sensitive feel for the real world both in and outside of the Christian Church. He approaches this effort at outreach with the same passion and practicality St. Paul did so many centuries ago. Too often, theological efforts are dull and difficult for anyone but scholars to be interested in. This book has the potential to arouse a new excitement among many who have never considered the real story of Jesus, the Messiah.

REV. TIM SEEBER, PASTOR, ZION LUTHERAN CHURCH, KALAMAZOO, MI

LORD OF LEGENDS

Jesus' Redemption Quest

ERIC T. EICHINGER

CONCORDIA PUBLISHING HOUSE • SAINT LOUIS

DEDICATION

To Michael Kossen, who instilled in me an appreciation for superheroes, and Todd Stryd, with whom I enjoyed many trips to the comic book shop.

Published by Concordia Publishing House
3558 S. Jefferson Avenue, St. Louis, MO 63118-3968
1-800-325-3040 • cph.org

1   2   3   4   5   6   7   8   9   10   31   30   29   28   27   26   25   24   23   22

TABLE OF CONTENTS

FOREWORD by Rev. Dr. Paul L. Maier 5

PREFACE 9

INTRODUCTION 13

CHAPTER 1: An Extraordinary Origin Story 23

CHAPTER 2: A Salvific Calling 33

CHAPTER 3: Patience before Passion 43

CHAPTER 4: An Ominous Crossing 53

CHAPTER 5: Appointment with the Preparer 61

CHAPTER 6: Fortitude, Fellowship, and Fiends 69

CHAPTER 7: A Necessary Horror 81

CHAPTER 8: Enduring the Curse 89

CHAPTER 9: A Marvelous Godsend 97

CHAPTER 10: Return from the Abyss 105

CHAPTER 11: Phoenix Rising 115

CHAPTER 12: A Homecoming Gift 127

EPILOGUE 135

AFTERWORD 139

ACKNOWLEDGMENTS 146

BIBLIOGRAPHY 147

W hat is the most impressive and common theme or plot in epic or adventure literature? Clearly, it runs something like this: A hero is confronted with challenges seemingly impossible to surmount; nevertheless, the hero does so, winning the battle, defeating his enemies, or even dying, if he must. However, his funeral is so magnificent that the hero becomes the victor anyway, as does Achilles in Homer's *Iliad*. Readers never seem to tire of the legendary in stories of the hero and the problems he must surmount, whether these are recited by bards around an ancient campfire or holding the attention of today's young readers in a comic book. No matter how impossible these tales seem to be, this plot line is the same in almost every novel today, as it has been for centuries. Small wonder that Joseph Campbell could entitle his book *The Hero with a Thousand Faces.*

The world's most widely read book, the Christian Bible, is itself full of compelling adventures of numerous heroes and heroines in both Old and New Testaments, not to mention the greatest hero of all: Jesus of Nazareth, the Son of God, the Savior. Why is Jesus so rarely regarded as the hero He certainly was? The Christian answer is that the legendary qualities of all the other human heroes could infect the reader's opinion of Jesus so that He would be demoted to a merely human status, though as the most courageous protagonist the world ever knew. The non-Christian response, like that of Campbell, is a general desire to have as little to do with Jesus as possible. Jesus knew the horrible details of His death before it happened. But He shares with great heroes of the past the triumph over the great obstacles in their paths. On the other hand, non-Christians concur that Jesus might be regarded as only a legend, or they are happy to include Jesus only in the legendary category of world heroes: a magnificent myth, but a myth nevertheless. And like Campbell, they give Him little or no notice in their writings. Even great defenders of the faith such as C. S. Lewis and J. R. R. Tolkien frequently use speaking animals to retell the Gospel accounts. Thus, a rather unnatural division has occurred when it comes to comparing Jesus to the other heroes and protagonists of the past and present.

Until now.

In these pages, Eric Eichinger, an author and Christian pastor, is himself something of a hero in taking on the task of explaining how Jesus differs from the fictional superheroes of the past and present. He possesses the benefit of a solid education in theological Christian scholastics and in the history of classical antiquity through childhood on. His mother, a veteran high school teacher of Latin, continues teaching the classics to this day. Eichinger is, indeed, the man for the job.

Eichinger immediately and successfully solves the chronological challenges: namely, the vexing problem of who copied from whom. Jesus lived more than seven centuries after Homer and Hesiod, who traditionally related the tales of the pagan gods of Greece and Rome, identifying their origins and areas of exploits. Hence, it is widely assumed that biblical writers were hopelessly indebted to them since both were purveyors of fiction not fact (as critics assumed). The devastating response to this assumption is sheer laughter. The origin of Rome in 753 BC (about the same time Homer and Hesiod were writing) was a time comparatively late in Hebrew history, when King Hezekiah ruled Judah, whereas Saul, David, and Solomon reigned three hundred years earlier. Moses, the ancient lawgiver, was even three or four centuries before them. Moreover, the stories of Greek and Roman mythology did not reach final form, in all of their accounts, until Ovid and his *Metamorphoses* or even Thomas Bulfinch's accounts in the 1860s. Jesus, a contemporary of Caesar Augustus, had no reason whatsoever to draw from Greco-Roman mythology. He drew, instead, from the deep well of predictions regarding the Messiah that preceded the classical mythmakers by millennia.

Communications in the ancient world were more impressive than usually credited. Not only was intercultural mingling between vastly different civilizations possible, but it has also been widely demonstrated, as shown by the incredibly distant journeys from Rome to India and farther, by the Silk Road to the Far East. Thank the Hebrews for their great gift to the world of monotheism, as well as for their invention of the seven-day week, well-known to both Greeks and Romans. The usual assumed direction of the Romans' influence on the Hebrews can very well be reversed. Thus, they had considerable knowledge of Hebrew culture.

The author's methodology in this book is to sum up the exploits of the ancient world and compare and contrast them with those of the Hero of heroes, Jesus Christ. In doing the latter, he provides a brilliant summary in each case drawn more from messianic prophecy from the Old testament than the New, which shows a cohesive account in itself and an excellent summary of the life of Jesus. The reason for the emphasis on Old Testament prophecy should be obvious from the discussion above.

But why limit this approach to the ancient world? What about the youth in our current culture? Alas, each younger generation seems less and less interested in the classics, but they are still impressed by the hero stories and movies that draw on them; thus, the author involves Superman, Batman, Spider-Man, and even the Karate Kid (ouch) in his comparisons. In the case of such comparisons, the overall superiority of the biblical heroes, especially the Hero Jesus, shines forth dramatically. Each such contrast adds to a growing theological analysis of the true Lord of legends.

Eichinger does not dodge difficult chapters in the life of Jesus, such as the problem of that controversial clause in the Creed, "He descended into hell," as part of the resurrection.

In each case where similar heroic episodes are compared between the pagan accounts and the biblical narratives, the superiority of the latter becomes clearly obvious in every category, such as credibility, character development, significance, conviction, and especially intrinsic importance. As noted above, Jesus, the infinite superhero, is easily the first in any culture to die and rise again!

This clearly makes for a cosmic difference between the Easter event and the return of Superman from the dead to save a comic franchise. For that reason, Eichinger reports details of the Lord of legends, the Hero of heroes, tracing an ancestry back to nothing less than creation itself. Indeed, the preexistent Jesus was also the Word, the Second Person of the Holy Trinity, existing before creation itself. His heroic story has no ending until His final return.

Finally, we might well ask, why is a book like this necessary, aside from the obvious intrinsic insights of this greatest-hero story? Eichinger comments regarding the dissatisfaction of the young with many aspects of church life today, especially including preaching, often with doctrinal themes that don't easily engage today's youth. Eichinger reveals a vast treasury involving hero themes and the great myths of the past with electrifying insights. God, in His permissive provenance, might well have allowed the victorious theme to pulse through literature, from the authors of ancient epics to motion picture screenplays, novels, and even comic books, to help an unbelieving world become more receptive to God's mission in saving the world through the greatest adventure of all in the story of the *Lord of Legends*.

—Paul L. Maier
Russell H. Seibert Professor of Ancient History
Western Michigan University
Author of *The Genuine Jesus: Fresh Evidence
from History and Archeology*

PREFACE

don't like going to church; it's boring." Many frustrated people have heard similar disheartening statements like that through the years, from children and grandchildren to spouses and close friends. If only Christianity and the Church could be more interesting or engaging. What if there were a connecting story thread woven through not just the Sunday morning hour but the entirety of the Church Year? What if this thematic saga was one not bloated in boredom, but in fact brimming with adventure? It is as if each Sunday service was another riveting chapter of a hero on a grand odyssey of atonement, bleeding grace into the very pages of our lives.

Jesus Christ is that hero. He is the ultimate adventure hero who not only rescues us but also saves the world in the process. Seeing Jesus as a hero does more than simply make Sunday mornings more interesting. Understanding Christ as the Hero of all heroes is a fascinating *tour de force* of the faith for all eternity. Exploring this incredible adventure is as easy as attending church this coming Sunday. If that's too challenging, no worries. Just keep reading.

Let's face it: faithfully going to church can be intimidating to some and daunting to others. Seemingly archaic rituals intertwined with ingrained traditions can feel suffocating to the newcomer, not to mention the nominal visitor. So much detail is woven throughout the service, it can be hard to absorb, understand, or process everything. This is a tall task for many children growing up in a liturgical worship context, as well as for the new person giving it a try. From the seasons of the Church to the high holy days, variant liturgy formats, challenging scriptural passages, and a non-visitor-friendly hymnal, many people can grow discouraged. The seeming lack of user compatibility may even cause many potential worshipers to punt on the Church and possibly Christianity altogether. For others, faith in Christ and regular worship, if kept, is often reduced merely to Christmas and Easter attendance. Any level of appreciation for Christian music reverts to only the popular Christmas carols, which are sung but once a year.

Christmas knowledge is actually a wonderful place to begin. It's virtually the origin of the greatest story ever told. The trick is realizing that Jesus' journey is like no other while at the same time it appears like so many hero stories our culture already adores. Like being pulled into a fascinating grand adventure novel, Christ deeply desires to engage everyone in His story. He wants everyone to be not only hearers of this story but actual participants as well. God's Word is alive, and it jumps off the page, for "the Word became flesh" (John 1:14). If you've come so far as to be familiar with Christmas, will you go a bit farther?

Advent, Christmas, Epiphany, the Baptism of Our Lord, Transfiguration, Lent, Palm Sunday, Maundy Thursday, Good Friday, Easter, Ascension, Pentecost. At one glance, these are the very obvious seasonal markers of the Church Year; at another glance, they are the magnificent plotlines of something much greater. The appointed Scripture readings for each Sunday throughout the year faithfully tell the story of the epic redemption quest of Jesus. Many people do not recognize all of these festivals. They either discard the whole lot of them, or they simply reduce their recognition of them to a brief nod for the "big two" of Christmas and Easter. Doing so guts so much of Christ's adventurous story. It is the equivalent of streaming the best scene or two from an Oscar-worthy film without relishing its entirety in full context and thus being profoundly moved.

What many do not realize is this annually celebrated pattern of Jesus' story is a didactic sequence, possessing all the major hallmarks of the stages of a classic hero's journey. Jesus' story is a generationally transcendent epic tale like no other, and it has the power to transform our lives. Trying to make sense of church for the unfamiliar is as easy as determining where in the story one is on any given Sunday. Entering a church for a newbie, no matter where the action picks up, is much like determining in which chapter, when, and where we last left our hero.

There are clues to follow. The sights and sounds of the Divine Service illumine the way. The number of candles lit and the seasonal colors of paraments accent the story. Our language in the liturgy and creeds of the faith routinely retraces Christ's glory story. Our creeds proclaim the identity of our triune God by telling His heroic story every time one is recited. Pastors, the knightly sages that they are, guide us week by week through a wilderness world with the torchlight of truth found only in the Word of Christ. The wisdom found in the weekly Scripture readings leads us through the transitions and progressions of Jesus' ultimate quest. We zoom in to one particular episode each week, which only grows richer year after year.

Our hymnody also sings of this adventurous sojourn. Christmas carols are wonderful, especially the most familiar ones, and yet they sing only of the mere beginning of the epic tale of Christ that He so desperately wants us to know. There are many other carols to know, enjoy, and love, as well as many other seasons: Advent carols, Lenten carols, Easter carols, and much, much more. The Church has its own timeless soundtrack of the epic story of salvation, made transcendent to our modern generations. We pilgrims of this age do ourselves a disservice if we ignore them. This life is too lonely and cold without the mercifully merry company of Christ in our midst.

INTRODUCTION

I f you could have a superpower, any superpower, which one would you choose? Many a passionate youngster has pondered this desperately important question over the years. Let's be honest: more than a handful of daydreaming adults have as well. It's a fun fantasy to explore on a slow day, and even better when stuck in a dire work setting with difficult people. The temptation of conjuring up an avenging superpower—if only you could—seems like the perfect answer, albeit fleetingly, to restore order quickly in one's life. The question remains: Which power would you select? Flight? Strength? Super speed? Time travel? Telekinesis? The list of possibilities goes on, ad infinitum.

This curious temptation traces all the way back to the Garden of Eden. The devil presented the false possibility of having godlike power to an innocent and unsuspecting couple.

> For God knows that when you eat of it your eyes will be opened, and you will be like God, knowing good and evil.
> (GENESIS 3:5)

For Eve, the choice was obvious. She scarfed down the seemingly fruitful opportunity, and together with Adam, she subsequently plunged humanity into a truly desperate situation.

When reduced to its simplest form, all temptation is essentially another lie by the Deceiver, enticing us to believe we can in some way become like God. If you simply do this, if you snidely reply that, if you follow a darker alternate path, you will be better. Your position will rise. Your unspoken craving will finally be satisfied as you achieve godlike status. For God must be holding out on you. Surely that is the only reasonable explanation of why life feels as unfulfilled as it does. Ascend, become His equal, and He no longer dictates His laws over you. Become your own god, and essentially you defeat Him. As hideous as it sounds, that is the empty promise on the back end of sin. However, the devil's lies never work out the way we think they will.

Ever since the fall into sin, humankind has sought a way to rescue itself from sin and its horrible consequences: despair, death, and damnation. Today, humanity still seeks innovative ways to work its way out of that same doomed dilemma. A savior is sought, but all too often is only searched for within one's heart. Consequently, an unhealthy messiah complex is born.

We desire a remedy for the sinful human condition, but because of our instinctive and self-perceived heroics, we also want to *be* the remedy. This futile quest takes us down dead-end trails. We elevate our personal powers of skill, knowledge, accomplishment, features, fame, or money to outlandish importance as we endlessly attempt to be the one doing the rescuing. We act as if our trivial triumphs will somehow redeem us. It is a Sisyphean struggle if there ever was one.[1]

At 30 Rockefeller Plaza in New York City, a magnificent sculpture appropriately graces the entrance. It is of Prometheus in his zenith, stealing fire from the gods to share with humanity. This gesture gifted a discontented humankind with the literal spark for all technology. The longing of the natural to possess the supernatural is almost as old as the rock we live on. Prometheus, while a demigod himself, was a champion for humanity. His fate serves as a fitting fable of caution for the consequences of humanity daring to possess divine power. He was chained to a rock, and a large bird arrived to rip out his liver, only to have it grow back, repeating the excruciating scenario each day for all of eternity. Lovely.

A savior is necessary to rescue humankind from the curse of sin, but no ordinary mortal or invented folklore will do. Only a true savior, a supernatural, divine savior, can save. Christ is that Savior, the God of gods, the Lord of lords, the King of kings, even the Hero of heroes.

---

1   In classic Greek mythology, Sisyphus, the king of Corinth, was sentenced to a most unique punishment. For his crimes of deceit and general arrogance, Zeus forced him to push an immense boulder up a great hill only for it to roll down every time it neared the top. The action was to be repeated for all of eternity.

Our culture loves its superheroes, as every respective culture has loved its own in ages past. Many examples of ancient Greco-Roman pottery contain some of the earliest hero images, such as decorative clay vases depicting mythological heroes in battle. These rudimentary comic book scenes decorated many a home throughout the Hellenistic world. We still enjoy our superheroes today, and yes, occasionally we even entertain illusions of being one. Inherently, we know we are broken and must be saved. The secret yearning we have of wanting them to be real compels us to reinvent them over and again. We enjoy hearing how good triumphs over evil, which feeds our irrepressible hope for the proverbial chosen one to someday actually arrive and save the world. We can't help but fancy ourselves as a hero in the narrative of our lives, perhaps even the superhero of our own personal mythology. There is no lack of material to borrow from.

The superheroes of today are our culture's modern mythology; they are recognizable stories reborn out of classical mythology. It is not too terribly difficult to link numerous contemporary superheroes with the Greek gods of antiquity. When examining characters such as the Flash, Wonder Woman, Aquaman, or Iron Man, one doesn't have to squint that hard to see strong similarities to Greco-Roman gods such as Hermes, Athena, Poseidon, or Hephaestus. The ancient and modern hero comparisons don't stop there. They are virtually endless.

Where do all these characters and stories come from? Why do the heroic themes of rescue and resurrection come up so frequently in hero storytelling? Could it be these literary tropes are so familiar because many of the classic hero stories trace back in some way, shape, or form to the actual, real, and true superhero, the Promised One Himself, the Savior, Jesus Christ? It is no accident that as the Gospel proclamation of Christ's resurrection spread, the heroic traits of a promised one, triumphant in battle to the death, who also miraculously rises to save the day, became increasingly prevalent themes for many would-be heroes.

Skeptics love to interject, saying the Greco-Roman gods predate Jesus by roughly seven hundred years.[2] Hence, how could Jesus influence those stories? While it is true many Greek mythology characters predate Jesus' earthly ministry, many of the more popular and recognizable myths known today weren't written until Roman epic poets embellished and added to the originals. Ovid's *Metamorphoses* and Virgil's *Aeneid* were written under none other than Caesar Augustus, who famously sent out a decree when Jesus was born.[3] Their later writings added a great deal to the initial legends, which have blended into the consciousness of today's foggy memory of antiquity. It is also true that Christ predates everything because He existed from the beginning. Moreover, He was prophesied to the first human beings in Genesis, recorded long before any Greek or Roman tomes were concocted.

It is quite plausible to discern how many stories from antiquity were conceived out of the biblical account of the Old Testament. During prehistory, stories were simply told around the fellowship of the fire, a gathering time for meal and conversation. Those who believed in Yahweh as the one true God had faith and understood that the stories were true historical events of human history. This context explains why the earliest stories of Genesis are fairly simple, straightforward, and repetitive accounts. They could be retold and remembered easily through generations by oral tradition.

However, time churned on toward a pivotal moment when telling stories became not so easy. After the language-scrambling episode of the tower of Babel, different people groups branched out. Over time, many of these people groups began to not believe in God—but they knew the stories. They remembered the stories of creation, the origin of humankind, and the fall. They recalled stories such as Genesis 3, which contains the first Gospel proclamation of the Messiah. God declared to the devil, "I will

---

2   The *Theogony*, which means "Birth of the Gods," is a poem written by Hesiod in the late eight or early seventh century BC. It is typically regarded as the most intact version of the Greek creation myths that survived that era.

3   The second chapter of Luke is one of the most famous Scripture passages of all time, and it is always read aloud during Christmas Eve services around the world.

put enmity between you and the woman, and between your offspring and her offspring; He shall bruise your head, and you shall bruise His heel" (Genesis 3:15). A Messiah will one day come and save. A Son of God and of mortal woman, one person, simultaneously man and God.

Throughout the generations, these truths of creation, the fall, and the promised Savior were passed down among God's people. These inspired words, preserved by the Holy Spirit, were eventually written down by Moses in the Book of Genesis.

But imagine a godless people, having played a "telephone game" mouth to ear for well over a millennium, hearing spoken stories around the fire, echoing through the generations, trying to come to terms with themes such as creation, sin, mortality, divine immortality, resurrection, and a vague promise of a God-man, a chosen one that one day would show up and restore all things.

It is a well-regarded belief that famed Greek writers and near contemporaries Homer and Hesiod used existing oral poetry and folklore to organize the framework for the Olympic pantheon of gods. An honest scholar would also recognize it is exceedingly believable they borrowed from familiar scriptural stories (oral poetry) and spoken Hebrew traditions (folklore) in their strident efforts to Hellenize surrounding cultures.

It is not too difficult to find evolved and blended stories of heroic gods and men and women reconciling a relationship with one another. The similarities are striking when cross-referenced with the early biblical account. Adam, who had dominion over all the earth and creatures (see Genesis 1:26), and Eve, the mother of all life (see Genesis 3:20), are great mystical literary prototypes for Zeus and Hera. They are virtually described in the same ways, respectively. As for a dark devil taking the form of a serpent, pick your poison from the various nefarious underworld characters: Hades, Calibos, Medusa, or perhaps the goddess Eris, who also managed to start a war by offering an "apple of discord." Zeus once even asked Poseidon, god of the sea, to flood the world because he was angry at humankind. Would Noah ponder plagiarism if given the opportunity?

Better still are the heroic Christ figures of ancient lore. Virgil unmistakably drew from the Book of Isaiah in some of his writings.[4] For thousands of years, classical antiquity carried portions of biblical truth and occasionally grafted in aspects of the prophesied Christ.[5] Hercules serves as a prime example. Hercules, the god-man, was born of god (Zeus) and mortal woman (Alcmene). He had to perform twelve tasks to be fully recognized and enter godlike status.

Variant hero stories have been rehashed and redeveloped time and time again, filtering down to our present generations. These epics, mere dim reflections of the one true story of Christ's death and resurrection, were reimagined so many times that a pattern emerged. This pattern was recognized and chronicled by a British author, Lord Raglan,[6] in his magnum opus, *The Hero: A Study in Tradition, Myth and Drama*, published in 1936.

Raglan's greatest contribution, the hero pattern, is a compiled list of traits by which any literary candidate must satisfy a number of qualifiers in order to be considered a true hero. His identified incidents that occur with regularity in the hero myths of all cultures amazingly list as follows:

1. The hero's mother is a royal virgin;
2. His father is a king, and
3. Often a near relative of his mother, but
4. The circumstances of his conception are unusual, and
5. He is also reputed to be the son of a god.
6. At birth an attempt is made, usually by his father or his maternal grandfather, to kill him, but
7. He is spirited away, and
8. Reared by foster-parents in a far country.
9. We are told nothing of his childhood, but

---

4   Virgil's Eclogue 4 is often referred to as a messianic poem by later Christian scholars. It predicts the birth of a boy that will bring a new golden age of peace. Virgil clearly had in mind the offspring of his friend Caesar Augustus, but the uncanny messianic prediction language caught the strong attention of many Christians years after, notably Constantine, Augustine, and Dante.

5   Psalm 2; 16:8–11; Isaiah 52:13–53:12; Daniel 7:13–14.

6   Fitzroy Richard Somerset, 4th Baron Raglan (1885–1964), was a British soldier, author, and amateur anthropologist.

10. On reaching manhood he returns or goes to his future kingdom.

11. After a victory over the king and/or a giant, dragon, or wild beast,

12. He marries a princess, often the daughter of his predecessor, and

13. Becomes king.

14. For a time he reigns uneventfully, and

15. Prescribes laws, but

16. Later he loses favor with the gods and/or his subjects, and

17. Is driven from the throne and city, after which

18. He meets with a mysterious death,

19. Often at the top of a hill.

20. His children, if any, do not succeed him.

21. His body is not buried, but nevertheless

22. He has one or more holy sepulchres.[7]

Remarkably, yet perhaps unsurprisingly so, Christ meets every single qualifier in either His divine nature or human nature. Lord Raglan, rather dismissive of Jesus Christ as the one true God, amusingly disagreed. While Lord Raglan did give Jesus credit for ticking many of the twenty-two boxes of hero prerequisites, he focused his primary attention elsewhere, toward other literary heroic characters. Here are how some of the more prominent heroes scored on Raglan's chart:

Moses (20)	Beowulf (15)
Romulus (19)	Zeus (14)
King Arthur (19)	Samson (13)
Perseus (19)	Achilles (10)
Hercules (17)	Odysseus (8)

Roughly a century ago, a conversation was brewing about a similar topic. The discussion took place between a Christian named John and a non-Christian who went by the name of Jack. Both learned men loved

---

7   Lord Raglan, *The Hero: A Study in Traditions, Myth and Drama*, reprint edition (Mineola, NY: Dover Publications, 2011), 174–75.

literature and writing, and they both celebrated a strong appreciation for mythology. One evening on a stroll together, John asked Jack if he believed in God. Jack, bitter from his experience in the Great War (World War I), said he did not. John pressed on further, suggesting the mythology they both cherished contained portions of truth, stemming from a greater truth in God, in fact, in Christ. Over time and more conversation about the potential of John's *true myth* concept, Jack ultimately came to faith in Christ. Both men went on to write tremendous literary treasures of humanity. Their renown is better recognized by their authorial names: J. R. R. Tolkien (John) and C. S. Lewis (Jack).

Their works, particularly stories in the realm of fantasy, have helped shape much of Christian thinking in the last century in terms of the supernatural interacting with the natural world, allegorical of how God redeems humankind. Tolkien published *The Hobbit* in 1937 and wrote *The Lord of the Rings* through much of the 1940s. Lewis gifted the world with *The Chronicles of Narnia*, publishing his first offering, *The Lion, the Witch, and the Wardrobe*, in 1950.

Across the pond in America, at roughly the same time, another literature professor had been studying the pioneers before him in the subjects of mythology and comparative religion. Fascinated with the seemingly endless similarities, Joseph Campbell refined his theory of the archetypal hero and is typically credited with coining the word *monomyth*, as well as his generationally insightful "hero's journey" story arc. Campbell published *The Hero with a Thousand Faces* in 1949, and our pop culture of hero storytelling has never been the same. Just ask George Lucas.

The most recent adaptation of the hero's journey storytelling technique is probably the most influential on our present generation. In his book *The Writers Journey: Mythic Structure for Writers*, first published in 1992, Christopher Vogler condensed Campbell's work and made it palatable for modern audiences. It provided a straightforward template that has become industry standard for hero storytelling (see the chart on the forthcoming page).

So many of these familiar hero stories, both ancient and modern, appear to contain splinters of truth broken off from the cross of Christ crucified. Jesus, however, is not merely another myth on the fantasy shelf in the library. His story is in fact—history! Christ's redemptive sojourn is the singular source of all hero stories, a *mono-truth*, if you will.

This book explores the glory story of Jesus through the framework of an epic hero. It is in the familiar storytelling language our culture has grown accustomed to. The redemptive quest of Jesus will be examined in the Scriptures through the iconic steps of a classic hero and will resonate with how present-day minds have been honed to hear about heroes. And so, we begin exploring Jesus: the Lord of legends.

The Hero's Journey [8]

- Ordinary World
- Call to Adventure
- Refusal of the Call
- Meeting with the Mentor
- Crossing the Threshold
- Tests, Allies, Enemies
- Approaching the Inmost Cave
- The Ordeal
- Reward (Seizing of the Sword)
- The Road Back
- Resurrection
- Return with the Elixir

8   Christopher Vogler, *The Writer's Journey: Mythic Structure for Writers*, 25th anniversary edition. Reprinted courtesy of Michael Wiese Productions (www.mwp.com).

AN EXTRAORDINARY ORIGIN STORY

In the beginning was the Word, and the Word was with God, and the Word was God.

—JOHN 1:1

et me tell you a story. It begins far outside our solar system. A father, under perilous circumstances, sends his only son to earth. The infant is taken in by a kind and unsuspecting couple. The child possesses talents well beyond the abilities of mortals. He grows up and becomes the champion for truth and justice. The world has never seen someone quite like him before and marvels at his power. Some love him, others hate him.

Intriguingly, he has a dual identity. He is entirely human in appearance and at heart, raised and cultured by human parents. He appreciates and cares for all the same values and concerns. Yet at the same time, he is also greater than human, almost godlike in stature. He is truly a mysterious hero—a savior from beyond the stars—come from the heavens to rescue the planet. He carries the weight of the world on his shoulders. He is even willing to sacrifice all of himself for the sake of humanity. During one notable incident, he surrenders himself to death for a sad season, only to return triumphant and victorious over the villain, to the astonishment of all.

Who is this super man, might you ask?

If you said, "Superman," you are both correct and incorrect at the same time. While this origin story is explicitly about Superman, it is also strikingly recognizable on a deeper, more profound level. When comic book creators Joe Shuster (artist) and Jerry Siegel (writer) brought this character to life in the pages of *Action Comics* #1 (1938), there was also an unintentional yet undeniable underlying parallel story. The readily obvious root source of this story is none other than Jesus Christ.

Shuster and Siegel were both Jewish by heritage. While they were aware of Jesus, faith in Him would have been considered blasphemous to their faith culture. They certainly did not deliberately intend to connect Superman with Jesus. So how did they end up tying one into the other so clearly? Could the Jewish belief in the coming messiah have played a role in how they formed Superman? As Jewish men, they believed in a coming messiah, and on whatever level of personal faith, they hoped one day he would actually come. This intrinsic hopefulness likely played a subconscious role in forming Superman into a caricature of what the messiah might be like. As creatives, this artistic projection reinforces the subtle yet irrefutable impact of Christ's glory story upon humanity's psyche, Christian or not. Jesus as the ultimate epic hero affects humankind's storytelling, in the conscious and even the subconscious. This had to come from somewhere.

THE ORDINARY WORLD

Every great hero or heroine[9] must start someplace, an ordinary world from which to launch. What are his roots? Where did she come from? The ordinary world is the basic surrounding and circumstances that make up each hero's personal distinctiveness. Perhaps the hero comes from poverty or wealth. Perhaps he comes from a distant planet, within a mountain, or under the sea. Perhaps he dwells in the misery of tragic loss or the majesty of mighty royalty. Perhaps she is an only child, the eldest, the youngest,

9   From this point, the term *hero* will stand for both hero and heroine.

or an orphan hopelessly lost in the shuffle. The ordinary world serves as the backdrop before the hero's adventure starts and the journey of his or her character arc begins. The ordinary world speaks greatly of what a hero is like and suggestive of what he or she might become.

One of the more beloved worlds in literary fantasy is J. R. R. Tolkien's vivid creation of the Shire, where hobbits bask in utopian peace with an abundance of food, drink, song, and safety. Who wouldn't want to hang out cozily for a visit and a meal? The ordinary world is the origin story of the hero. It helps color the ensuing adventure and makes us appreciate the full arc of the hero even more. Eventually, the hero arrives on the scene, and inquiring minds want to know just exactly who this person is and whence they came.

Jesus burst onto the scene with wisdom such as no one had heard before. He spoke in parables, dropping truth bombs that stunned the status quo of thinking. Once His ascent of notoriety began to take off, the questions of Jesus' origin came flying in fast and furious.

> And coming to His hometown He taught them in their synagogue, so that they were astonished, and said, "Where did this man get this wisdom and these mighty works? Is not this the carpenter's son? Is not His mother called Mary? And are not His brothers James and Joseph and Simon and Judas? And are not all His sisters with us? Where then did this man get all these things?" And they took offense at Him. But Jesus said to them, "A prophet is not without honor except in his hometown and in his own household." (MATTHEW 13:54-57)

Once the ordinary world of Jesus' hometown was discerned as Nazareth, people definitely had their rather telling opinions.

> Philip found Nathanael and said to him, "We have found Him of whom Moses in the Law and also the prophets wrote, Jesus of Nazareth, the son of Joseph." Nathanael said to him, "Can anything good come out of Nazareth?" Philip said to him, "Come and see." (JOHN 1:45-46)

THE ORIGIN STORY OF JESUS

The true origin story of the hero Jesus is, as you might suspect, not so simple. We will have to probe deeper than many might first realize. After all, there is Jesus' origin, and there is also Christ's origin. Before your brain begins to throb, here again Superman's origin serves us a helpful, glimmering hint. Superman possesses dual citizenship. He has his adoptive parents, Ma and Pa Kent, from Smallville, though by way of his previous address, planet Krypton. Similarly, Jesus has two natures, human and divine, with complementing origins.

If we begin with the human nature of Christ (Jesus in the flesh), some initially started to recognize Jesus as the potential Messiah and peppered Him with questions. Where did this man come from? What of Jesus as a boy? Let's retrace His steps and see what we might find.

As ludicrous as it sounds, Jesus most likely did not notably stand out in His youthful coming-of-age years. He surely blended in amidst the attitude of "Look how special our perfect little angelic child is," typical within the parenting world. Consequently, there were plenty of other children to "come and adore" in the neighborhoods of Nazareth. The prophet Isaiah even foretold of Him in this unassuming way:

> He grew up before Him like a young plant, and like a root out of dry ground; He had no form or majesty that we should look at Him, and no beauty that we should desire Him.
> (ISAIAH 53:2)

While the boy Jesus was divine, perfect, and sinless in every way, He still managed to give an occasional headache to a nervous parent. One account in the Gospel of Luke details a borderline "Amber Alert" situation when He seemingly went missing.

> After three days they found Him in the temple, sitting among the teachers, listening to them and asking them questions. And all who heard Him were amazed at His understanding and His answers. And when His parents saw Him, they were

astonished. And His mother said to Him, "Son, why have You treated us so? Behold, Your father and I have been searching for You in great distress." And He said to them, "Why were you looking for Me? Did you not know that I must be in My Father's house?" And they did not understand the saying that He spoke to them. And He went down with them and came to Nazareth and was submissive to them. And His mother treasured up all these things in her heart. And Jesus increased in wisdom and in stature and in favor with God and man. (LUKE 2:46–52)

The only other biblical post-infant episode of Jesus is recorded during the visit of the Wise Men. Jesus was two years old at most upon their arrival. The visit of the Magi was mysterious in a variety of ways and serves as an epiphany concerning Jesus' origin. The Magi (from which we get the word *magician*) were scholarly men who studied astronomy. They most likely heard of the prophecies of the coming Messiah from Israelites in Babylonian captivity. Ultimately, they set out to find this Savior come from beyond the stars. The Magi, in their quest to worship Him, believed that the child was not just a king but also divine.

After Jesus was born in Bethlehem of Judea in the days of Herod the King, behold, wise men from the east came to Jerusalem, saying, "Where is He who has been born king of the Jews? For we saw His star when it rose and have come to worship Him." (MATTHEW 2:1–2)

The Magi did not show up empty-handed. They brought belated birthday presents for Jesus. The gifts of gold, frankincense, and myrrh accented the suggestion of Jesus' royalty (gold) and also inadvertently suggested His imminent death (burial perfume).

Then Herod, when he saw that he had been tricked by the wise men, became furious, and he sent and killed all the male children in Bethlehem and in all that region who were two years old or under, according to the time that he had ascertained from the wise men. (MATTHEW 2:16)

Certainly, no origin story of a hero would be complete without his birth. Backtracking still further, we find the classic Word-becoming-flesh moment at Christmas.

> In those days a decree went out from Caesar Augustus that all the world should be registered. This was the first registration when Quirinius was governor of Syria. And all went to be registered, each to his own town. And Joseph also went up from Galilee, from the town of Nazareth, to Judea, to the city of David, which is called Bethlehem, because he was of the house and lineage of David, to be registered with Mary, his betrothed, who was with child. And while they were there, the time came for her to give birth. And she gave birth to her firstborn son and wrapped Him in swaddling cloths and laid Him in a manger, because there was no place for them in the inn. (LUKE 2:1–7)

The shepherds and angels would soon fill in and complete the nativity scene. The shepherds no doubt went repeating the sounding joy, going and telling on the mountain of the angelic prophecy that a Savior had been born. However, if we are faithfully holding ourselves accountable to Jesus' true origin story—life technically begins at conception. Perhaps Christmas should not be celebrated so much as the Annunciation, when the angel Gabriel gave Mary the big news and a gender reveal party to boot.

> In the sixth month the angel Gabriel was sent from God to a city of Galilee named Nazareth, to a virgin betrothed to a man whose name was Joseph, of the house of David. And the virgin's name was Mary. And he came to her and said, "Greetings, O favored one, the Lord is with you!" But she was greatly troubled at the saying, and tried to discern what sort of greeting this might be. And the angel said to her, "Do not be afraid, Mary, for you have found favor with God.

> And behold, you will conceive in your womb and bear a son, and you shall call His name Jesus. He will be great and will be called the Son of the Most High. And the Lord God will give to Him the throne of His father David, and He will reign over the house of Jacob forever, and of His kingdom there will be no end." And Mary said to the angel, "How will this be, since I am a virgin?" And the angel answered her, "The Holy Spirit will come upon you, and the power of the Most High will overshadow you; therefore the child to be born will be called holy—the Son of God." (LUKE 1:26–35)

Jesus' divine nature was referenced specifically and corroborated by the angels at His conception and birth, all the while being born of a virgin maiden. Jesus was no ordinary child. His ordinary world was anything but ordinary; it was indeed extraordinary. He was royal yet lowly, divine yet human, full of life yet with an ominous death looming.

Just in case you thought the origin of Jesus was complete, push the pause button. It's Ancestry.com time. There are not one but two distinct genealogy lines attributed to the birth of Jesus. Matthew 1:1–16 follows the line of Joseph, Jesus' legal father. It begins with Abraham[10] and ends with Jesus, for the benefit of the Jewish people, inquisitive of Jesus' royal lineage.

Luke's Gospel genealogy is for the benefit of the Church, already believing Jesus is the Son of God. It begins with Jesus the son of Joseph and concludes with the source of His lineage, Adam, who was "the son of God" (Luke 3:38). Like Father, like Son. If Jesus is the Son of God, didn't He exist from the dawn of time? Great question.

---

10   The great patriarch with whom Yahweh made a covenant that he would be the father of a great nation.

CHRIST'S ORIGIN STORY

Flying to our aid one last time, Superman, much like Christ in His origin story, has an earthly home as Clark Kent. However, he also possesses a deeper origin as Kal-El, from the planet Krypton. He is alien to the world we know. He even conveniently gets his superpowers from the light of the sun. This dual nature of Clark Kent and Superman is helpful in understanding the two natures of Christ.

While the human nature of Jesus was conceived by the Holy Spirit and born of the virgin Mary roughly two thousand years ago, Christ was always the Son of God, there from the beginning. Each nature of Christ had its unique origin, as the Athanasian Creed says, "He is God, begotten from the substance of the Father before all ages; and He is man, born from the substance of His mother in this age" (v. 29; *LSB*, p. 320).

The evangelist John writes in vivid detail of how the one person of God in Christ Jesus is reconciled.

> In the beginning was the Word, and the Word was with God, and the Word was God. He was in the beginning with God. All things were made through Him, and without Him was not any thing made that was made. In Him was life, and the life was the light of men. The light shines in the darkness, and the darkness has not overcome it. (JOHN 1:1–5)

If one reads through the text above and replaces "the Word" with "Christ," immediately the hypostatic union[11] becomes crystal clear. God became man, forever. In context, John 1:14 plants a flag of emphasis with the line "The Word became flesh."

The Nicene Creed[12] helpfully articulates the faith this way:

---

11   A theological term used to describe the personal union of Christ's humanity and divinity once permanently combined in His one individual existence.

12   The Nicene Creed is a statement of faith used in Christian liturgy. Its name comes from the city of Nicaea, where it was adopted at council as a Church confession in AD 325.

I believe in one God, the Father Almighty, maker of heaven and earth and of all things visible and invisible. And in one Lord Jesus Christ, the only-begotten Son of God, begotten of His Father before all worlds, God of God, Light of Light, very God of very God, begotten, not made, being of one substance with the Father, by whom all things were made. (*LSB*, p. 158)

Jesus articulated this at one point in His ministry: "And now, Father, glorify Me in Your own presence with the glory that I had with You before the world existed" (John 17:5). Christ was there, in the heavenly realms, united in the Trinity from before time began. Christ was always God but was not always man. He did not become man until He took up human nature as Jesus.

Any aspiring hero would not be a true hero unless something is accomplished. Superman would have never lived up to his name had he not actually done something super. A hero must be called into the right context to perform some heroic act. So, too, with Christ; a special calling would occur, and He would set aside His divine power and glory and come down out of the heavens.

> God the Father, light-creator,
> To Thee laud and honor be.
> To Thee, Light of Light begotten,
> Praise be sung eternally.
> Holy Spirit, light-revealer,
> Glory, glory be to Thee.
> Mortals, angels, now and ever
> Praise the holy Trinity![13]

---

13   "Thy Strong Word," *LSB* 578:6 (© 1969 CPH).

CHAPTER

2

A SALVIFIC CALLING

He shall bruise your head, and
you shall bruise His heel.

—GENESIS 3:15

I t was shaping up to be a wonderful evening for the young boy. He exited the theater into the alleyway with his two doting parents. The three of them laughed and merrily discussed the show they had just witnessed. It was a night he would never forget. The boy wondered what else the evening might hold for him as they walked. Ice cream, or perhaps a quick stop at the candy store would make the night perfect. But any childlike fantasies he clung to quickly faded away. A gunman stood before them. Two shots reverberated through the side streets, only muted by Lucifer-like laughter. The gunman fled with his spoils from the wealthy couple, and young Bruce Wayne had heartbreakingly stumbled upon his call to adventure. The soon-to-be Batman vowed vengeance against all criminals. He would be a valiant Dark Knight in the shadowy corners of society where the light of justice rarely shined. The career for the crime-fighting Caped Crusader was born.

THE CALL TO ADVENTURE

A call to adventure thrusts a hero into action. It can be an exciting lure, or a perilous necessity, or some blended combination of the two. The hero-to-be is in his or her ordinary world, perhaps content, perhaps discontent. Eventually, a summons of some fashion stirs the hero to depart from the known to the unknown. The call to adventure can be by invitation, or it can be a choice with which the character must wrestle. In other instances, as in Batman's story arc, a tragic event befalls that ominously sets the stakes. It compels the hero to take up the task or begin the quest.

What is at stake must be critically important to the hero. It might revolve around family and friends, romance and rescue, treasure or truth, or the necessity for executing justice. The list is endless. The greater the stakes, the greater the adventure. The hero must care enough about the stakes not merely to begin the quest but also ultimately to complete it. Heroes often rise and fall on their personal motivations. Their calling bares a vocational sense of duty or obligation. The strength of their sense of calling is often in direct relationship to the stakes involved.

Jesus has a certain calling, though *adventure* is hardly the word to describe it. God had created the world and all that is in it. Everything was good and pleasing to Him, perfect and holy in every way. Creation was crowned with the masterpiece of humankind, created in the very image of God. Adam and Eve resided in the Garden of Eden, basking in the splendor of God's presence.

Yet not long after creation occurred, tragedy struck. With Satan's temptation, Adam and Eve disobeyed God's command and ate of the fruit of the tree of the knowledge of good and evil. Consequently, all of creation became contaminated with that original sin. Their initial disobedience plumed into a mushroom cloud of cosmic proportions. The entire system of the cosmos had become polluted with wickedness. Just as God foretold, if they ate of it, they would surely die, they and all of creation. Worse yet, everyone forever after would inherit the same penalty and be cursed to eternal damnation in the fires of hell. Something needed to be done.

The Greek word πρωταγωνιστής gives us the English word *protagonist*. It translates literally as the "first agonizer." The protagonist hero of any story is the first to take up the cause, agonizing in pursuit of resolving the conflict. Conflict is always central to drama. A struggle of some sort ensues; humankind against nature, human against human, or human against God. Often, an inner struggle of the hero accompanies the outer struggle, providing a richly layered character.

Christ is the first agonizer for humankind's dilemma of sin. He cares deeply for His people and does not want them to bear the consequences of sin—namely, death. It is God's divine inner struggle. Yet the outer struggle remains. Humanity has sinned; therefore, humanity must die. Christ, the Word of God, is called to remedy this problem and endure agony in the process.

And so, the advent of Jesus, our King, began. The stakes could not be any higher. God was not about to let His wonderful creation drift off into the chasm of condemnation—not without a fight. A Champion would be sent, but not just any hero would do.

THE CHOSEN ONE

In rare occurrences, the call to adventure for a hero hinges on a destined prophecy. Only a certain chosen one can fulfill the need. A mysterious summoning oracle foretold from long ago, echoed through generations, awaits a particular individual to arrive in triumph. This chosen one who is to come is a specific person, solely capable of meeting the moment and achieving the task. The concept of a predestined chosen one is a unique call to adventure. The hero is a one-of-a-kind figure, exclusively fit to match the need of the pressing conflict.

In our world, Jesus is this figure, and for all applied purposes, He is the Chosen One. Perhaps more specifically appropriate, Jesus is "the Anointed One." His designation, *Messiah* in Hebrew and *Christ* in Greek, both mean "the Anointed One." He is the one who comes to save, to make right what once went wrong, and to restore all things. Jesus is emphatically cognizant of this as He quotes from the prophet Isaiah while reading at the synagogue.

> The Spirit of the Lord is upon Me, because He has anointed Me to proclaim good news to the poor. He has sent Me to proclaim liberty to the captives and recovering of sight to the blind, to set at liberty those who are oppressed, to proclaim the year of the Lord's favor. (LUKE 4:18–19; SEE ISAIAH 61:1–2)

Christ's assignment was no reactionary measure of God the Father. The necessity of Jesus' mission and purpose was not some afterthought or patch to correct the unforeseen downfall of God's prototype creation. Christ's redemption quest had been preordained from the beginning of time.

> You were ransomed from the futile ways inherited from your forefathers, not with perishable things such as silver or gold, but with the precious blood of Christ, like that of a lamb without blemish or spot. He was foreknown before the foundation of the world but was made manifest in the last times for the sake of you who through Him are believers in God, who raised Him from the dead and gave Him glory, so that your faith and hope are in God. (1 PETER 1:18–21)

The omniscient foreknowledge of God was on full display already in the third chapter of Genesis. Here we find the *protoevangelium*, a Greek word that means the "first Gospel" proclamation.

> I will put enmity between you and the woman, and between your offspring and her offspring; He shall bruise your head, and you shall bruise His heel. (GENESIS 3:15)

These menacing words of doom, pronounced to Satan, hint at the only hope for humankind: the Promised Seed, Jesus Christ.

The particular redemption mission to which Jesus is called is literally to save the world—the entire cosmos of creation, down to the very last iota. The rescuing work asked of Christ was not for the faint of heart. He was called to be a sacrifice for the sin of the entire world.

Isaiah, among many prophets, repeated the promise of the One to come. Moreover, Isaiah foretold of the explicit reason for the coming of the Messiah. What awaits this Chosen One to come is described in menacing detail in this epic passage:

> But He was pierced for our transgressions; He was crushed for our iniquities; upon Him was the chastisement that brought us peace, and with His wounds we are healed. All we like sheep have gone astray; we have turned—every one—to his own way; and the LORD has laid on Him the iniquity of us all. He was oppressed, and He was afflicted, yet He opened not His mouth; like a lamb that is led to the slaughter, and like a sheep that before its shearers is silent, so He opened not His mouth. By oppression and judgment He was taken away; and as for His generation, who considered that He was cut off out of the land of the living, stricken for the transgression of My people? And they made His grave with the wicked and with a rich man in His death, although He had done no violence, and there was no deceit in His mouth. Yet it was the will of the LORD to crush Him; He has put Him to grief; when His soul makes an offering for guilt, He shall see His offspring; He shall prolong His days; the will of the LORD shall prosper in His hand. Out of the anguish of His soul He shall see and be satisfied; by His knowledge shall the righteous one, My servant, make many to be accounted righteous, and He shall bear their iniquities. Therefore I will divide Him a portion with the many, and He shall divide the spoil with the strong, because He poured out His soul to death and was numbered with the transgressors; yet He bore the sin of many, and makes intercession for the transgressors.
>
> (ISAIAH 53:5–12)

Bruce Wayne had to heed the call to become Batman. He would not allow the evil of crime to perpetuate in the streets any longer. If Batman never swooped in, countless innocent lives might be permanently damaged or destroyed. He could not allow those consequences to take place in the absence of his future actions of justice. Similarly, God had to act.

Humankind sinned against God and neighbor, and humanity therefore stands condemned to eternal death and hell. It is the age-old problem with no simple answer. Restitution is needed. Since humanity has inherited responsibility for its sin, it seems only just that humanity must pay for those sins. It is the greatest conundrum for humanity. Humankind cannot talk, pay, or work its way out of this penalty. The solution of rescuing all of humanity from sin would be an ever-so-delicate one. To accomplish this, it would mean Christ must leave the heavenly realms and come to earth. This is what Christ was called to do, as He was sent by His Father.

Intriguingly, the root word for *hero* comes from its Greek origin, ἥρως, which means "to protect or defend." Martin Luther described the meaning of the First Article of the Apostles' Creed in this way: "He defends me against all danger and guards and protects me from all evil."[14] One major way God accomplished this, out of His Fatherly divine goodness and mercy, was that He sent His only Son to suffer and die in the place of humanity.

Later in Jesus' earthly ministry, on several occasions He articulated the reasons why He was sent. He made it abundantly clear He had come by directive of His Father. This call by God the Father makes a strong distinction from Jesus acting of His own initiative. Jesus clarified He was on a divine errand from heaven, sent by God the Father. "For I have come down from heaven, not to do My own will but the will of Him who sent Me" (John 6:38). Another time He said, "If God were your Father, you would love Me, for I came from God and I am here. I came not of My own accord, but He sent Me" (John 8:42).

Jesus not only illuminated that He was sent, but He also established the reason for His coming—to save the people. The people did not easily recognize this. Jesus stated that He came that they might see, to be their light, to bear witness to the truth: "I have come into the world as light, so that whoever believes in Me may not remain in darkness" (John 12:46).

---

14   Luther's Small Catechism, First Article.

The Gospel of Luke offers another instance: "And Jesus said to [Zacchaeus], 'Today salvation has come to this house, since he also is a son of Abraham. For the Son of Man came to seek and to save the lost'" (Luke 19:9–10).

It goes without saying that these are not the simplest concepts for sinful, prideful people to absorb and digest. Jesus did not simply come in peace to make everyone feel good about themselves and remain as they are. He came with truth. Jesus' truth is Good News—in fact, it is the finest news there ever is to hear. To those who reject His truth, it would seem Jesus comes bearing a sword and judgment. Certain prominent New Testament quotes from Jesus follow:

> Do not think that I have come to bring peace to the earth. I have not come to bring peace, but a sword. (MATTHEW 10:34)

> Jesus said, "For judgment I came into this world, that those who do not see may see, and those who see may become blind." Some of the Pharisees near Him heard these things, and said to Him, "Are we also blind?" Jesus said to them, "If you were blind, you would have no guilt; but now that you say, 'We see,' your guilt remains." (JOHN 9:39–41)

> Then Pilate said to Him, "So You are a king?" Jesus answered, "You say that I am a king. For this purpose I was born and for this purpose I have come into the world—to bear witness to the truth. Everyone who is of the truth listens to My voice." (JOHN 18:37)

GOD "RETCONS" HIS UNIVERSE

When God the Father calls Christ to earth, He bids Him come and die. Through His death, humankind has a new pathway forward, one not of death but of life—an eternal life, as God originally designed humankind to enjoy. "I came that they may have life and have it abundantly" (John 10:10).

Occasionally, in rare beloved literature, characters will come along that transcend generations. After passage of time, another writer may come along with new story lines for said adored characters to travel down. Often in these instances, the existing audience despises the new direction of the story arc. They feel betrayed, as if the new direction of the story has deviated from the original source material in such a profound way that the entire franchise is ruined. In such literary crises, a *retcon*, meaning a *retroactive continuity*, is in order. An amending retcon dismisses the new material as inconsequential, salvages the characters, and returns to the foundation of the story.

God the Father created the world with intentionality. He desired for humankind to live in His holy presence forever. However, the devil steered humanity, God's beloved characters, off the perfect path of God. Satan, an interloper of the creative narrative, deceived Adam and Eve and all their descendants into sin and despair. Sin changed the story line regarding humankind's ultimate ending from one of innocence to a reality of corruption, death, and hell. God in Jesus Christ orchestrated one massively divine retcon to redeem all the world.

Christ's death would rewrite and erase the causative sin of the devil's lies, creating a new reality, one in which humankind once again enjoys life everlasting, as God originally intended. For Jesus to pay for the sins of the world in His own death would mean the possibility of a course correction for everyone throughout all of time. Lest Satan forget, Christ is the author of life.

That is quite a call to adventure for the hero who is Jesus Christ. Christ is called to die, but the quest does not end there. Thankfully, the prophecy of the messianic Chosen One also says something more: "For You will not abandon my soul to Sheol, or let Your holy one see corruption" (Psalm 16:10).

How might this all be reconciled? We must not travail, attempting to explain the interrelationship of the Trinity. Perhaps the best way to understand Christ's undertaking is in the way God describes it Himself:

For God so loved the world, that He gave His only Son, that whoever believes in Him should not perish but have eternal life. For God did not send His Son into the world to condemn the world, but in order that the world might be saved through Him. (JOHN 3:16–17)

When a hero receives a call to adventure, there is more than one answer to consider:

> The advent of our King
> Our prayers must now employ,
> And we must hymns of welcome sing
> In strains of holy joy.[15]

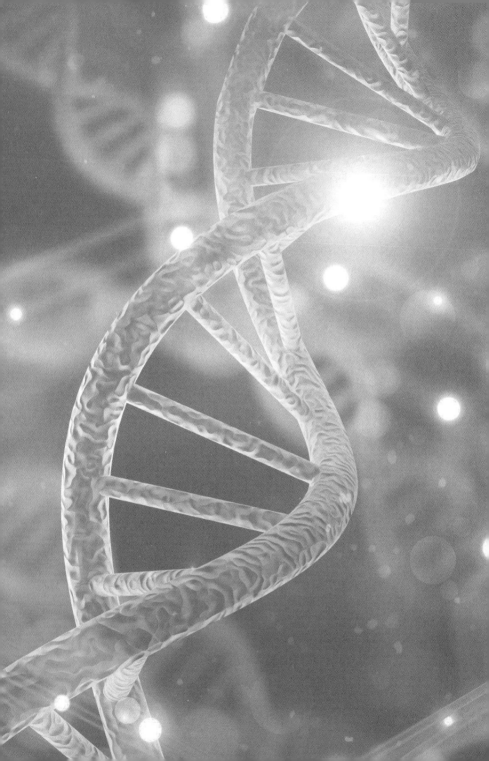

PATIENCE
BEFORE PASSION

The spirit indeed is willing, but the flesh is weak.

—MATTHEW 26:41

Essentially—"With great power comes great responsibility!" Many a novice superhero enthusiast will quickly attribute that axiom to Spider-Man. A truer fanboy might even diligently point out that Spider-Man, alternatively known as Peter Parker, didn't actually say the famous line. Rather, his beloved mentor figure, Uncle Ben, said it to him. In actuality, when Spider-Man first appears, in *Amazing Fantasy* #15, no specific character is credited with that powerful proverb of dialogue. It is written in the narrator box on the last panel.

Peter Parker is torn by a dilemma after he is bitten by a radioactive spider in a science lab. He could either use his newfound abilities for the greater good of society or remain within his own obscurity, relishing in teenaged selfishness. He chooses the latter, with great repercussions. Given the option of easily stopping a criminal running from the police, Peter shrugs off the act. Soon after, he discovers Uncle Ben has been murdered by that very criminal. Peter vows never to avoid helping again whenever possible, and Spider-Man is born. The assertion that with great power there must also come great responsibility remains a thematic touchstone of purpose for him ever after. The saying essentially serves as Spider-Man's constant reminder of his initial refusal of the call.

REFUSAL OF THE CALL

The refusal of the call to adventure typically happens almost immediately after receiving the call. As the potential hero realizes the immense danger that lies ahead, trepidation sets in. Not every hero refuses the call. Some do not have an option. They are thrust into a new context independent of their own actions. It may be an accident or a passive outer source that leads an individual into the situation. Regardless, the only option is to move onward. Yet more often than not, a budding hero is faced with a choice: follow the path of least resistance and safety, or forge forward into the mysterious unknown.

When a hero-to-be refuses the call, it is usually only for a short season. A situation quickly arises that prompts the consideration to reverse course and enter the fearsome fray. Forbearing reluctance plays a strong role as a hero wrestles within himself or herself. When a hero eventually realizes that answering the call is the only obvious path forward, it provides much exposition for what might lay ahead.

The exposition scene of any great epic likely highlights the villain and reveals the plan to vanquish him or her. Be it a Minotaur, a dragon, Dr. Doom, the White Witch of Narnia, or Voldemo—excuse me, the one who shall not be named—an evil enemy is clarified. Hope rests in the hands of the hero and the plot to stop the adversary. The *antagonist* causes the source of agony for the protagonist. The adversarial antagonist struggles against the hero.

For Jesus, and for all the people of the world, the enemy goes by many different names. Satan, the serpent, Lucifer, Beelzebub, Deceiver, Belial, the Great Dragon, the Prince of Darkness. He is the devil, and he seeks to kill, destroy, and conquer. The only hope for the world rests in the hands of Christ. With great power there must also come great responsibility.

One might even argue that axiom comes from Jesus. His parable of the faithful servant sounds strikingly similar. "Everyone to whom much was given, of him much will be required, and from him to whom they entrusted much, they will demand the more" (Luke 12:48). Jesus seems always to have something powerful up His proverbial sleeve.

SUPERPOWERS

Superhero powers are always fascinating to ponder. Which powers complement or potentially neutralize those of another? Whose superpower would prevail in a conflict? When God's superpowers are considered, they are often succinctly summed up in our trinitarian creedal language: creation and blessings, justification and forgiveness, and sanctification and making holy. The powers of God in Christ Jesus, on the other hand, are much more mesmerizing upon deeper study.

Christ Jesus is at the same time both human and divine. This union of human and divine in one person conveys different attributes respectively. Each nature's attributes are equally important for Christ's mission of atoning sacrifice. God by Himself could not die. Humanity alone could not prevail over death. Either single nature alone would be void of meaning. However, the sole person of Jesus Christ receives a double essence of the two natures and thereby possesses the exclusive ability to conquer death eternally.

Furthermore, Christ's performance of miracles is exemplary as well. He maintains a monopoly on the supernatural venturing into the natural world. Jesus is one person acting through two natures. When He heals a blind man, His divine nature is extended through His human nature. He smears His own muddied saliva as some sort of supernatural salve, and the blind man miraculously is able to see (John 9:6–7).

The majesty of Jesus is that His human nature receives from His divine. The divine needs nothing from the human. The human nature participates with the divine as the divine works through it. In this way, Jesus is able to walk over water or pass through a wall to appear to His disciples. He is both true God and true man at the same time. He is omniscient, omnipotent, and, post-ascension, even omnipresent. Jesus has power in spades, and He needs no lectures about responsibility.

Two of the greatest responsibilities of any man are the vocations of father and husband. "For in Christ Jesus you are all sons of God, through faith" (Galatians 3:26). Christ possesses a paternal characteristic as well as one of matrimony. "Husbands, love your wives, as Christ loved the church and gave Himself up for her" (Ephesians 5:25). The parent-child connection and the institution of marriage are two profound relationships that God utilizes to help convey His relationship to us. He loves His people and seeks to save them at all cost, to the point of the ultimate sacrifice.

Consequently, it would be ludicrous to suggest that Jesus ever refused the call of His quest. Jesus chose not to refuse the call. However, a couple of Jesus' later episodes cause one's spider-sense to tingle.[16] The reader of the Scriptures must pause and grapple with some distressing words of Jesus.

REMOVE THIS CUP

> On the third day there was a wedding at Cana in Galilee, and the mother of Jesus was there. Jesus also was invited to the wedding with His disciples. When the wine ran out, the mother of Jesus said to Him, "They have no wine." And Jesus said to her, "Woman, what does this have to do with Me? My hour has not yet come." His mother said to the servants, "Do whatever He tells you." (JOHN 2:1–5)

This seems like a mild request of a mother, who knows her son well, to perform a simple task. Yet this sequence is rich with nuance. Readers often fail to recognize the magnitude of the situation at first glance. The details of a wedding, in Galilee, on the third day, and water turning into wine were not mere happenstance. Even Mary, who appears to be not entirely

---

16   Peter Parker's "spider-sense" is one of Spider-Man's most unique powers. A tingling sensation occurs in the back of his head immediately before a hazardous situation arises, offering a split second of consideration before acting.

naive of what Jesus is capable, most likely did not fully comprehend what was about to spring forth from her maternal entreaty.

Mary is met with a slight rebuff from Jesus. "Woman, what does this have to do with Me? My hour has not yet come" (v. 4). This is unexpected behavior from a son to a mother, and particularly from the Son of God. If only the tone in His voice could be known.

Typically, a call refusal for a hero will come at the beginning of the journey. While Jesus has already been human for some time, this event stands on the precipice of Jesus' earthly ministry. Once Jesus begins to perform miracles for people to see, particularly His disciples, it starts a countdown clock of events that will not stop until He breathes His last breath on Calvary. It's as if Jesus had all this in mind, savoring one last moment of festive peace before everything would change. Seemingly no sooner than He alludes He won't involve Himself with the present situation, He commits to the task.

> Now there were six stone water jars there for the Jewish rites of purification, each holding twenty or thirty gallons. Jesus said to the servants, "Fill the jars with water." And they filled them up to the brim. And He said to them, "Now draw some out and take it to the master of the feast." So they took it. When the master of the feast tasted the water now become wine, and did not know where it came from (though the servants who had drawn the water knew), the master of the feast called the bridegroom and said to him, "Everyone serves the good wine first, and when people have drunk freely, then the poor wine. But you have kept the good wine until now." This, the first of His signs, Jesus did at Cana in Galilee, and manifested His glory. And His disciples believed in Him. (JOHN 2:6–11)

It became abundantly clear to the servants and Jesus' disciples that this rabbi was like no other. While cups of wine were being filled full, Christ was fulfilling much of the Old Testament. The fact that this event also happened on the third day of the wedding is appropriate; the phrase "on the third day" is distinctive, often used in the Bible during divine revelation.

A few foreshadowing revelations are of Moses and Elisha, who respectively took their turns making bitter water sweet (see Exodus 15:22–25; 2 Kings 2:19–22). Also, the prophets Isaiah and Amos each spoke of the coming of the Messiah in conjunction with the abundance of wine (see Isaiah 25:6–9; Amos 9:13–15).

All this in the context of a wedding feast in Galilee is more than perfect—it was divinely appointed. For this was a double wedding of sorts. When Christ performed His first miracle at Cana, He essentially bound Himself as the Husband to His people, the new Israel, the Bride of Christ. He as the Bridegroom unified Himself to the Church, His Bride, through that first miracle. Christ did not refuse the call. This Groom of grooms didn't have cold feet, but He did express an appropriate level of patience before His Passion. His hour had not yet come.

It is noteworthy to point out that Jesus' mother, Mary, only makes two appearances in the Gospel of John. She is present at the wedding at Cana and at the crucifixion, where water and wine/blood are both poignantly thematic. Another captivating pairing of Jesus' first miracle is with the first of God's ten plagues in Egypt, where water is turned to blood. It is all the more enthralling when we consider that Jesus' last miraculous act on the cross matches the last of the ten plagues: the death of the firstborn son.

Christ's hour would soon enough be upon Him, and He would be sweating it out, though with a different cup being referenced:

> And they went to a place called Gethsemane. And He said to His disciples, "Sit here while I pray." And He took with Him Peter and James and John, and began to be greatly distressed and troubled. And He said to them, "My soul is very sorrowful, even to death. Remain here and watch." And going a little farther, He fell on the ground and prayed that, if it were possible, the hour might pass from Him. And He said, "Abba, Father, all things are possible for You. Remove this cup from Me. Yet not what I will, but what You will." And He

came and found them sleeping, and He said to Peter, "Simon, are you asleep? Could you not watch one hour? Watch and pray that you may not enter into temptation. The spirit indeed is willing, but the flesh is weak." And again He went away and prayed, saying the same words. And again He came and found them sleeping, for their eyes were very heavy, and they did not know what to answer Him. And He came the third time and said to them, "Are you still sleeping and taking your rest? It is enough; the hour has come. The Son of Man is betrayed into the hands of sinners." (MARK 14:32–41)

While this event transpires at the twilight of Jesus' earthly ministry, and not toward the beginning as typical of a refusal of the call, it certainly raises strong questions from the reader about the text. Was Jesus unwilling to die for the sins of the world? If it is not His will, does He still love us? Does this somehow cheapen what Christ was about to do at Calvary?

As odd as it may sound, this conflicted state of Jesus can actually be a source of comfort to the Christian. Our prayers do not fall on deaf ears. We have a God in Christ who understands pain, suffering, and death. His body physically braced for the agony He knew full well was coming. This highlighting of His humanity lets any and all know that He gets us. Jesus understands our human suffering on an intimate and personal level. He was not about to lean easily on His divine nature and die meaninglessly on a cross sans the suffering. This chapter of Jesus' journey speaks volumes. As terrifying an ordeal as death by crucifixion would be for us to face, that is exactly what Jesus had to endure. He palpably felt the distress, just as much as the next person would.

If the Gospel of Mark uses a wide-angle lens on this episode, the Gospel of Luke employs a zoom-in focus with a popular biblical literary technique called a *chiasm*. Chiastic structure employs a mirroring effect of bookend references within a passage, layered with emphasis toward the center and thus the heart of the matter. The center focus of this story in Luke is Jesus' words "Father, if You are willing, remove this cup from Me. Nevertheless, not My will, but Yours, be done" (Luke 22:42).

It is hard to underscore the gravity of Jesus' petition. "The whole purpose of Jesus' ministry, and of the Gospel, is at stake in this request."[17] In the shortest of moments, everything in the universe could have been so easily unhinged with a single word.

Yet Christ pressed on from the tender moment of fragile love. It left humanity with an ever-increasing appreciation of the precious value of what Christ was about to do. Ultimately, Jesus knew He had an ordained destiny from heaven above. God gave Jesus a call He couldn't refuse. Jesus answered the call. He was sent to die a willing sacrificial death for the sins of the world.

> With might of ours can naught be done,
>> Soon were our loss effected;
> But for us fights the valiant One,
>> Whom God Himself elected.
> Ask ye, Who is this?
> Jesus Christ it is,
>> Of Sabaoth Lord,
>> And there's none other God;
> He holds the field forever.[18]

17   Arthur A. Just, *Luke 9:51–24:53*, Concordia Commentary (St. Louis, MO: Concordia Publishing House, 1997), 859.

18   "A Mighty Fortress Is Our God," *LSB* 656:2.

CHAPTER
4

An
Ominous
Crossing

The Word became flesh.

—JOHN 1:14

I t was supposed to be a simple game of hide-and-seek. Four siblings scoured through a mysterious mansion on a rainy afternoon in search of the perfect hiding spot. The youngest of the four thought she had spied the best location. A large wooden wardrobe in a lonely room would envelope her well, she figured. She stepped inside and was met by a solidly packed bunch of fur coats. Sibling voices down the hallway prodded her forward. She pushed and forged her way through the thick layers, stepping back deeper into the wardrobe than she thought possible. To her astonishment, she found herself standing in a winter forest of snow-covered trees. She could see her chilled breath. The warm, inviting light from a random lamppost beckoned her forward. Lucy Pevensie had arrived in Narnia.

CROSSING THE THRESHOLD

The first time Lucy passed through the magic wardrobe, fans of the classic story instantly became captivated.[19] She crossed a threshold into a new realm, an enchanted land of spiritual manifestation. A tantalizing adventure awaited her. There could be no turning back.

When the threshold has been crossed, it signals the adventure has begun. The hero is committed, regardless of what might happen. The threshold may be a portal of some kind, a vehicle or spaceship, or even a rudimentary looking wall concealing a certain platform 9¾. Regardless, the way to bypass the barrier of separation between the hero's ordinary world and the extraordinary is revealed. Passage through is finally made possible. An adventurous quest in a new world looms, pregnant with possibilities.

For God to come to earth, no magic wardrobe, secret train, or Millennium Falcon would do. He had a different means of transportation in mind. Gabriel's angelic announcement to Mary ensured that. Christ crossed the threshold when He took upon Himself human flesh and brought humanity into the Godhead permanently. While Jesus resided in the temporal home of His mother, an eternal reality was taking shape. When Christ passed through the safe vessel of a virgin's womb, it was a one-way ticket. The dawn of a new era was nearly ready to shine forth, forever.

While Jesus silently grew inside, Mary gave words to her distinctive condition.

> My soul magnifies the Lord, and my spirit rejoices in God my Savior, for He has looked on the humble estate of His servant. For behold, from now on all generations will call me blessed; for He who is mighty has done great things for me, and holy is His name. And His mercy is for those who fear Him from generation to generation. He has shown strength with His arm; He has scattered the proud in the thoughts of their hearts; He has brought down the mighty from their thrones and exalted those of humble estate; He has filled

19   C. S. Lewis, *The Lion, the Witch and the Wardrobe.*

the hungry with good things, and the rich He has sent away empty. He has helped His servant Israel, in remembrance of His mercy, as He spoke to our fathers, to Abraham and to His offspring forever. (LUKE 1:46–55)

The ominous crossing of Christ from heaven into the sinful world was drawing nigh. The Good News of forgiving grace was that much closer to physical reality, which begged a big question. How would all these promises be accomplished?

ALWAYS WINTER, NEVER CHRISTMAS

Not until Lucy and her siblings, all four of the Pevensie children, came through the wardrobe did events begin to churn into motion in *The Lion, the Witch, and the Wardrobe*. Soon after they all arrived, the advent of their adventure became evident. For countless years, the citizens of Narnia had endured the hardship of "always winter and never Christmas" under the treacherous rule of the White Witch. Yet the youth were told that because of their arrival, "Aslan is on the move."[20] Aslan, the kingly Christ-figured lion, was apparently on his way to restore all things under his reign.

Something changed when Jesus came to the world. God was on the move. The Old Testament gave way to the New. The chronic season of deathly winter, which had been a sinful world yearning for a Savior, melted with the Messiah's birth. Christ descended from the heavenly celestial realm when Mary conceived Him by the power of the Holy Spirit. Naturally, nine months later, Jesus was ushered into a manger in Bethlehem.

And she gave birth to her firstborn son and wrapped Him in swaddling cloths and laid Him in a manger, because there was no place for them in the inn. And in the same region there were shepherds out in the field, keeping watch over their flock by night. And an angel of the Lord appeared to them, and the glory of the Lord shone around them, and

---

20   C. S. Lewis, *The Lion, the Witch and the Wardrobe* (New York: Harper Collins, 1950), 19, 78.

they were filled with great fear. And the angel said to them, "Fear not, for behold, I bring you good news of great joy that will be for all the people. For unto you is born this day in the city of David a Savior, who is Christ the Lord. And this will be a sign for you: you will find a baby wrapped in swaddling cloths and lying in a manger." And suddenly there was with the angel a multitude of the heavenly host praising God and saying, "Glory to God in the highest, and on earth peace among those with whom He is pleased!" (LUKE 2:7–14)

That first Christmas was a sacred event. Christ's arrival in the flesh of Jesus was of universal importance. The Prince of Peace had come to contend with the prince of this world, Satan. The first Christmas, and every Christmas since, means that the warm light of hope for all humankind is real and visible. The people who had been living under the cold darkness of sin and death now have reason for joy. "The people who walked in darkness have seen a great light; those who dwelt in a land of deep darkness, on them has light shone" (Isaiah 9:2).

Humanity can't help but draw near to this precious infant king and the Good News He has to bring: forgiveness and righteousness. As a result, Christmas can be experienced every day in the midst of a fallen world. Knowing Jesus is an enchantingly warm, shelter-like experience, in which God meets humanity in the bitter, soul-freezing winter of sin.

In Jesus Christ, God's presence, magnificence, and otherwise overwhelming power and glory became man. Concealed within the precious nature of an infant, God connects with humankind on a most tender and intimate level. He draws close to our hearts in the form of a gentle little child. The Creator becomes part of His creation: Christ Jesus, the Word made flesh. "And the Word became flesh and dwelt among us, and we have seen His glory, glory as of the only Son from the Father, full of grace and truth" (John 1:14).

Another way to translate this particular verse is "the Word became flesh and *tabernacled* among us." The tabernacle was the fragile tent of meeting for the Israelites in the Old Testament. It was a temporary temple pointing to a permanent one. It was also a place where sacrifices were made and God interfaced with humankind. All of these details are significant to keep in mind when John references the imagery of a tabernacle in his description of God in the flesh. God, in Jesus' fragile tent of flesh, was certainly pointing to a more permanent, everlasting temple of His resurrected body. This would be accomplished by His ultimate sacrifice, all while He interfaced with humankind.

Jesus is not some distant God from on high who is completely out of our comprehension. He is relatable in a comforting way. The Word became incarnate and shares intrinsic commonalities with us. Jesus is the inexplicable familiar foreigner to all wanderers of this world.

During travel, an instant connection is felt when one discovers a complete stranger from a shared hometown. It can have a disarming effect. The Word becoming flesh conveys a shared experience on a profound level. Because God became man, He knows the same landmarks of pain and suffering that we know. He's walked the same side streets of sadness and alleyways of anguish familiar to sinners of a sinful world. Jesus understands poverty and pain, hunger and thirst, the loss of a beloved friend, even death itself. That is the very purpose of why He crossed the threshold in the first place: to suffer in our place and die the death we should have on account of our sin.

AN ALTAR EGO

Heroes often possess a second self, an alter ego, or alternate version of themselves. This secret identity conceals their true identity. Prominent examples range from outlandish leotard-fitting outfits with loud colors, capes, and masks to simply wearing glasses and parting one's hair on the opposite side of the head. A hero may choose to wear a disguise for a variety of reasons: the shock of a loved one finding out the hero puts himself in constant danger, the increased hazard if her cover is blown, or the mounted pressure put on his regular identity. Therefore, an alter ego is created. It allows the hero to operate with others in two different capacities.

Jesus is God, veiled in flesh. While He is entirely human, He is also entirely divine. God in human form as a mortal being is not a simple concept for the average Joe to absorb, nor for the average Joseph in Jesus' day. God in Christ Jesus has an *alter* ego, but in His specific case, an *altar* ego would be more accurate.

While Jesus is fully human in every observable way, He has an alter ego: He is God. Yet He also has an altar ego: He is the Messiah, come to die a sacrificial death. The expectation of the people for the role of the Messiah was not the same as what God intended. The people sought a messianic king to rule politically. Christ would indeed rule, but His kingdom was not so readily obvious to the public physical world. It remained hidden, even to this day. Not until His final return on Judgment Day will His rule be visibly evident to all. Jesus would exercise His kingdom reign in a way not of this world. Christ's altar ego meant that God the Father would sacrifice Him on the altar of the world to pay for the sins of the world. An ordinary human can give nothing in exchange for his or her soul. Yet the one true God-man, Jesus Christ, can provide everything via His vicarious atonement for all of humanity.

From time to time, a particular hero's secret identity may be discovered, alluded to, or revealed on purpose. Jesus predicted His death on several occasions to His disciples, but they either could not understand His cryptic messaging, "Destroy this temple, and in three days I will raise it up" (John 2:19), or they refused to entertain the notion:

> And Peter took Him aside and began to rebuke Him, saying, "Far be it from You, Lord! This shall never happen to You." But He turned and said to Peter, "Get behind Me, Satan! You are a hindrance to Me. For you are not setting your mind on the things of God, but on the things of man."
> (MATTHEW 16:22–23)

During a revealing point in His ministry, Jesus chose to uncloak His divine nature to some of His disciples. On the Mount of Transfiguration, Jesus met two Old Testament figures, long since gone, yet miraculously alive in the moment.

> Now about eight days after these sayings He took with Him
> Peter and John and James and went up on the mountain to
> pray. And as He was praying, the appearance of His face was
> altered, and His clothing became dazzling white. And behold,
> two men were talking with Him, Moses and Elijah, who
> appeared in glory and spoke of His departure, which He was
> about to accomplish at Jerusalem. (Luke 9:28-31)

The transfiguration is both a miracle and a mystery in the ministry
of Jesus. His divine nature is revealed and then concealed again. Only a
precious trio of Jesus' disciples were "eyewitnesses of His majesty" (2 Peter
1:16). Oftentimes, when a hero's identity becomes known to one or a small
group of individuals, there are implications. The information is typically
protected. Such was the case here. "And a voice came out of the cloud,
saying, 'This is My Son, My Chosen One; listen to Him!' And when the
voice had spoken, Jesus was found alone. And they kept silent and told
no one in those days anything of what they had seen" (Luke 9:35–36).
They would not be able to begin to process what they had seen for a while
later, after the resurrection.

In Jesus, God crossed over the threshold, from heaven to earth, in order
to become a threshold for a greater purpose. "I am the way, and the truth,
and the life. No one comes to the Father except through Me" (John 14:6).
Christ became the portal for the sinner to pass through into a different
realm, a new world as a new creation. "I am the door. If anyone enters by
Me, he will be saved and will go in and out and find pasture" (John 10:9).
Once Christ crossed the threshold into the flesh, His mission had only
just begun. A wild winding path was waiting to unfold before Him.

> "From heav'n above to earth I come
> To bear good news to ev'ry home;
> Glad tidings of great joy I bring,
> Whereof I now will say and sing."[21]

---

21   "From Heaven Above to Earth I Come," *LSB* 358:1.

APPOINTMENT WITH THE PREPARER

Behold, I send My messenger, and
he will prepare the way before Me.

—MALACHI 3:1

Luke Skywalker was in major trouble. He needed a lot of help. One of his newly purchased droids had wandered off on account of his irresponsibility. During his search, he was attacked and robbed by the violent, desert-dwelling Sand People. All this with a posse of stormtroopers coming down on him in pursuit of the droids. Luke also maintained a pesky yearning for something more in his life, yet a satisfying answer remained undiscernibly elusive.

Enter Obi-Wan Kenobi.

This hooded sage is shrouded with intrigue as he rescues Luke from immediate peril and ushers him back to safe lodgings. Thereupon, Obi-Wan imparts wave after wave of mentoring wisdom to Luke: the religiosity of the Jedi knights, the practice of the Force, and keen information about Luke's seemingly dead father at the hands of a mysterious foe—Darth Vader. The urgent request from a beautiful princess on a distant planet all but ensures dangerous wars among the stars will result.

MEETING OF THE MENTOR

The meeting of the mentor is a watershed moment for any hero. It is a vital relationship, through which a mentor figure equips the hero. The mentor may offer instruction, insight, resources, or some variant combination. Often, a talisman object of supernatural qualities is given: a weapon, a wand, a secret map, or armor. Typically, the hero meets the mentor early in the journey, though the timeliness of the mentor's appearance varies from epic to epic. The mentor may arrive in the hero's ordinary world or somewhere on the journey soon after the threshold has been crossed. The mentor might accompany the hero on the journey, stay in constant contact, or remain an overriding source of inspiration to the hero throughout the quest.

Jesus has left His ordinary world of heaven. He has grown up into adulthood. He is just about ready to begin His earthly ministry, but He is in need of a particular service. A critical christening must happen first before He launches.

Enter John the Baptist.

> There was a man sent from God, whose name was John. He came as a witness, to bear witness about the light, that all might believe through him. He was not the light, but came to bear witness about the light. The true light, which gives light to everyone, was coming into the world. He was in the world, and the world was made through Him, yet the world did not know Him. (JOHN 1:6–10)

John functions as the proverbial mentor, but in a slightly inverted way. He is not the classic figure shining with polished stateliness; far from it. He is quite the opposite as an outspoken wilderness wanderer, dressed in camel hair and with a suspicious diet of locusts and honey. Furthermore, Jesus is not some empty vessel waiting to be filled. Jesus does, however, have a specific requirement from John before He goes any farther along on His journey. John prepares the way for Jesus, despite his suggestive destitute appearance.

Often, a hero will have some prior awareness of the mentor character before their critical meeting. Luke knew of the old hermit, Ben Kenobi, before their encounter. Jesus and John were relatives, distant cousins with a foreshadowed ordainment when their paths first intersected. This providential interaction took place when they were both in utero. Mary, expectant with Jesus, visited her much older relative, Elizabeth, who was also pregnant with John.

> In those days Mary arose and went with haste into the hill country, to a town in Judah, and she entered the house of Zechariah and greeted Elizabeth. And when Elizabeth heard the greeting of Mary, the baby leaped in her womb. And Elizabeth was filled with the Holy Spirit, and she exclaimed with a loud cry, "Blessed are you among women, and blessed is the fruit of your womb! And why is this granted to me that the mother of my Lord should come to me? For behold, when the sound of your greeting came to my ears, the baby in my womb leaped for joy. And blessed is she who believed that there would be a fulfillment of what was spoken to her from the Lord." (LUKE 1:39–45)

Mary, a virgin, and Elizabeth, an elderly woman well past natural childbearing years, both had miraculous happenstance surrounding the conception of their respective sons. Neither of them had any natural business being pregnant, and yet God utilized them for a greater purpose. Jesus and John's relationship was established at the very beginning with mirrored juxtaposition. This would continue as Jesus drew nearer to His appointment with the preparer. John even said early in his ministry, "After me comes He who is mightier than I, the strap of whose sandals I am not worthy to stoop down and untie. I have baptized you with water, but He will baptize you with the Holy Spirit" (Mark 1:7–8).

THE GIVING OF A GIFT

Among training exercises, lessons, or clarifying secret knowledge, the mentor figure often will bestow a gift upon the growing hero. Obi-Wan Kenobi famously gives Luke Skywalker an heirloom of his birthright. When Luke picks up his lightsaber and wields his weapon for the first time, he takes a major step toward his future. John the Baptist, in mentor-like fashion, provides a major tool of necessity for Jesus—Baptism. All the while, John is acutely aware of the absurdity of the situation unfolding before him.

> Then Jesus came from Galilee to the Jordan to John, to be baptized by him. John would have prevented Him, saying, "I need to be baptized by You, and do You come to me?" But Jesus answered him, "Let it be so now, for thus it is fitting for us to fulfill all righteousness." Then he consented. And when Jesus was baptized, immediately He went up from the water, and behold, the heavens were opened to Him, and He saw the Spirit of God descending like a dove and coming to rest on Him; and behold, a voice from heaven said, "This is My beloved Son, with whom I am well pleased." (MATTHEW 3:13–17)

When Jesus received His Baptism, the heavens split open. God tore a rift in the sky, through which the Spirit of God descended upon Jesus in the form of a dove, and a voice from the Father spoke over Him. A trinitarian theophany[22] in all its glory. This monumental occurrence signaled direct access to God for whoever might be washed in Baptism thereafter.

Jesus was and remains without sin. He did not have to be baptized for the reason people are baptized today. When sinners are baptized, they become associated with God and all of His holiness. Forgiveness of sins is delivered by the power of God, through the water and His Word. When Jesus received His Baptism, He already possessed all the attributes

---

22   *Theophany*, an "appearance of God," is when the Trinity reveals itself to humankind in the Scriptures.

of God. Forgiveness of sin was not needed, for He had no sin to begin with. Rather, Jesus was baptized for a far greater purpose than His own individual requirements.

The Baptism of Christ made it so that all waters might be a rinsing away of sin through the baptismal ceremony. Jesus' perfect life lived under the Law of God set up a pivot from the Old Testament into the New Testament. When Jesus was baptized, He who is holy became united with all sinners. Henceforth, when sinners are baptized in the name of the Father, the Son, and the Holy Spirit, they become united with divine holiness. Jesus' Baptism lastingly identified Him with wickedness in order for future sinners to be everlastingly identified with God through their own Baptism. He sanctified baptismal waters as a Means of Grace so that all may have full assurance of forgiveness. The future hope of the world hung in the balance.

TO FULFILL ALL RIGHTEOUSNESS

Obi-Wan Kenobi also urged the vital need for Luke to begin his quest. It was necessary that Luke go to the distant planet Alderaan at the request of a beautiful princess and learn the ways of the Force. Luke's fateful meeting with Obi-Wan Kenobi crystalized the entire purpose of the mission and Luke's future. After all, the fate of the galaxy was at stake.

It was necessary for John to baptize Jesus in order to fulfill all righteousness. No one else would do. He had been appointed by God to be the preparer of the coming of the Messiah. No one else could fulfill the prophecies. No one else could prepare the way of the Lord. No one else could make straight the path toward Christ. He alone was the voice of one calling in the desert, as foretold by the prophet Isaiah (see Isaiah 40:3).

John the Baptist was an incredibly dynamic figure. Crowds flocked to him and his refreshingly new message. The people had been excited. The notoriety John attracted eventually got the attention of the local ruler, Herod Antipas. He feared John, because John could sway the crowds with his influential words. Accordingly, Herod put John in prison.

The pupil-mentor relationship is a fluid one. Occasionally, during trying times, one or the other will quizzically wonder if the hero has what it takes to accomplish the task they both seek. During John's imprisonment, word came to Jesus, "Now when John heard in prison about the deeds of the Christ, he sent word by his disciples and said to Him, 'Are You the one who is to come, or shall we look for another?'" (Matthew 11:2–3). Jesus' return correspondence summarized all the miracles He was performing—healing miracles fitting to the messianic prophecies being fulfilled. It was clear. Jesus was indeed the Coming One.

Jesus then continued teaching the crowd and offered a cryptic insight into the deeper identity of John the Baptist. "From the days of John the Baptist until now the kingdom of heaven has suffered violence, and the violent take it by force. For all the Prophets and the Law prophesied until John, and if you are willing to accept it, he is Elijah who is to come. He who has ears to hear, let him hear" (Matthew 11:12–15).

John was set apart as the forerunner of Christ, but that's not all. He also had a mysterious distinction in this role as a type of second coming of the prophet Elijah. Elijah and John the Baptist somehow possessed a shared identity as a co-harbinger of the Messiah. The last of the Old Testament prophets, Malachi, prophesied an unusual verse some five hundred years after Elijah's ministry: "Behold, I will send you Elijah the prophet before the great and awesome day of the LORD comes. And he will turn the hearts of fathers to their children and the hearts of children to their fathers, lest I come and strike the land with a decree of utter destruction" (Malachi 4:5–6).

Ever since Malachi's prediction, scholars had been mindful of the coming of the Messiah affirmed somehow by the return of Elijah. Presumably lending to this thought was the fact that Elijah had gone to heaven in a chariot of fire and technically never died. Elijah also foreshadowed the resurrection of the Messiah when he raised back to life the dead son of a widow (1 Kings 17:17–22). In some unforeseen way, Elijah was supposed to reappear before this forthcoming Day of the Lord.

John the Baptist certainly looked the part. The Scriptures describe both Elijah and John as wearing a garment of camel hair with a leather belt tied around the waist. Yet it is an abnormal jump to assume from mere appearance John represented the return of Elijah. This is a fair point; however, Jesus concretely validated John by linking him to Elijah.

Jesus, having just been in the presence of Moses and Elijah, walked down the Mount of Transfiguration with three of His disciples. The disciples, seemingly mindful of the significance, didn't ask Jesus about Moses, but they did inquire about Elijah. "And the disciples asked Him, 'Then why do the scribes say that first Elijah must come?' He answered, 'Elijah does come, and he will restore all things. But I tell you that Elijah has already come, and they did not recognize him, but did to him whatever they pleased. So also the Son of Man will certainly suffer at their hands.' Then the disciples understood that He was speaking to them of John the Baptist" (Matthew 17:10–13).

John the Baptist, the preparer of the way of the Lord, had done his job. He fulfilled his role in setting Christ's ministry in motion. In the case of many mentors, their stories may not end with mere aid. Sometimes they must die, in some noble way, which furthers the path forward for the hero.

> But when Herod's birthday came, the daughter of Herodias danced before the company and pleased Herod, so that he promised with an oath to give her whatever she might ask. Prompted by her mother, she said, "Give me the head of John the Baptist here on a platter." And the king was sorry, but because of his oaths and his guests he commanded it to be given. He sent and had John beheaded in the prison, and his head was brought on a platter and given to the girl, and she brought it to her mother. And his disciples came and took the body and buried it, and they went and told Jesus.
>
> (MATTHEW 14:6–12)

> On Jordan's bank the Baptist's cry
> Announces that the Lord is nigh;
> Awake and hearken, for he brings
> Glad tidings of the King of kings![23]

---

23   "On Jordan's Bank the Baptist's Cry," *LSB* 344:1.

CHAPTER

6

FORTITUDE, FELLOWSHIP, AND FIENDS

I will make you fishers of men.

—MATTHEW 4:19

Slay the Nemean lion. Kill the Lernaean nine-headed Hydra. Subdue the Ceryneian hind.[24] Capture the Erymanthian boar. Clean the stables of King Augeas in a single day. Defeat the Stymphalian birds. Capture the Cretan bull. Fetch the flesh-eating mares of King Diomedes. Steal the belt of Hippolyta. Obtain the cattle of Geryon. Retrieve the golden apples of the Hesperides. Conquer Cerberus, the three-headed dog guarding the gates of Hades.

Hercules, the god-man, had his work cut out for him. The twelve labors assigned to him by his nefariously influential cousin, King Eurystheus, were the ultimate challenge of his strength. These tasks also served as penance for killing his own family in a violent rage. Hera, who hated Hercules from birth, had tricked him into doing so. If he accomplished

---

24   A mythological golden-horned stag-like creature, prized by the goddess Artemis.

these tasks, as some of the ancient poets claimed, then Hercules would have a shot at gaining full deity status and prove he was a hero.

TRIALS

Every hero has trials to endure. Tests must be passed upon which the validity of the hero's true nature is verified. Quite simply, a hero must demonstrate he or she is in fact heroic. People need to know. The cause of the challenges may arise by what seems to be accidental happenstance, by the need of the community cherished by the hero, or perhaps mystically assigned, as in Hercules' case by the Oracle of Delphi. More often than not, the hero's opponent is behind these tests. The overarching evil adversary typically has hatched some plot against the hero, playing the role of puppeteer.

After Jesus was baptized, He departed into the wilderness. The Spirit led Him there to be tempted by the devil. Jesus was amid wild animals and subject to the elements for well over a month. He also set in place a special self-imposed suffering. Jesus went without food, fasting for the entire time, all while the Tempter tempted Him. With the end of the forty days in sight, Jesus was in a physically weakened state of human exhaustion. It was at this point that the devil showed up with a climactic three-pronged thrust of concluding temptations.

> And after fasting forty days and forty nights, He was hungry. And the tempter came and said to Him, "If You are the Son of God, command these stones to become loaves of bread."
> (MATTHEW 4:2–3)

It is critical to recognize that Jesus' forty days of temptation was a microcosm of misery, akin to the Israelites' forty years of wandering in the wilderness. This connection is of paramount importance for Jesus, who was about to fulfill specifically what God's chosen people could not. He had to pass the trials and remain sinless in a desolate location. These trials of Christ mirrored the trials the Israelites faced during the exodus, predating any fabled Herculean effort by almost a millennium.

It perhaps seems unusual for Satan to tempt Jesus in this way. Where exactly is the sin in eating? Gluttony? Really? Satan's bid barely resembled a temptation, especially for a hungry man. Yet so much more was on the table. Hercules' twelve labors seem like simple checkers compared to the mental chess match Jesus had to calculate, considering infinite moves ahead and their eternal consequences. If Jesus couldn't stomach the suffering of fasting, how would He resist not caving to stronger temptation down the pike when those watching the crucifixion would ask Him to prove He was the Son of God by coming down from the cross (Matthew 27:40)?

Jesus rebuked Satan, "Man shall not live by bread alone, but by every word that comes from the mouth of God" (Matthew 4:4). Jesus quoted the very Word of God in His response. Jesus' response references the time the Israelites sinned by grumbling against the Lord, for they were hungry in the desert. God provided manna, bread from heaven, for them to eat. "And He humbled you and let you hunger and fed you with manna, which you did not know, nor did your fathers know, that He might make you know that man does not live by bread alone, but man lives by every word that comes from the mouth of the LORD" (Deuteronomy 8:3).

Where the Israelites had bellyached against the Lord in starvation, Christ had tamed His human hunger. Perhaps more relevant, the only other man without sin ever to be tempted was Adam in the Garden of Eden. That enticing temptation also concentrated on eating food. Once again, where man had failed, the Son of Man endured.

Jesus passed the first temptation.

> Then the devil took Him to the holy city and set Him on the pinnacle of the temple and said to Him, "If You are the Son of God, throw Yourself down, for it is written, 'He will command His angels concerning you,' and 'On their hands they will bear you up, lest you strike your foot against a stone.'"
> (MATTHEW 4:5–6)

This diabolic test asked Jesus to prove His identity, yet in doing so, He would have defeated the point and Himself in the act. The devil evidently tried to put Jesus in an impossible situation, which Jesus easily saw through. The Son of God is sinless and must remain sinless all the way to the cross. Jesus brilliantly offered an equally scriptural reply: "Again it is written, 'You shall not put the Lord your God to the test'" (Matthew 4:7). Jesus and the Father are both equally God. Jesus' answer was true both from the perspective of Himself to God the Father and is also true from the perspective of the devil toward Jesus. This would not be the last time Jesus would be asked to prove He is God.

Jesus also quoted the Word of God again with His answer. In the Book of Exodus, the Israelites found themselves thirsting like never before, and they became incensed toward Moses, asking if God was in fact with them or not. Moses ended up striking a rock, by God's command, and from the rock sprang refreshing water for the people to drink with delight. They named the place *Massah* and *Meribah*, to remind and remember they had *quarreled* and *tested* the Lord there (Exodus 17:1–7).

Jesus remembered, and He passed the second temptation.

> Again, the devil took Him to a very high mountain and showed Him all the kingdoms of the world and their glory. And he said to Him, "All these I will give You, if You will fall down and worship me." (MATTHEW 4:8–9)

Near the conclusion of the Israelites' forty years of wandering in the desert, they found themselves on the brink of the Promised Land. God gave statutes and rules to remember after they entered. Among fearing the Lord, loving Him, and teaching about Him to their children in all walks of life, God specifically described what they would see in the land:

> And when the LORD your God brings you into the land that He swore to your fathers, to Abraham, to Isaac, and to Jacob, to give you—with great and good cities that you did not build, and houses full of all good things that you did not fill, and cisterns that you did not dig, and vineyards and olive trees that you did not plant—and when you eat and are full, then take care lest you forget the LORD, who brought you out of the land of Egypt, out of the house of

slavery. It is the LORD your God you shall fear. Him you shall serve and by His name you shall swear. You shall not go after other gods, the gods of the peoples who are around you.
(DEUTERONOMY 6:10–14)

The cities, houses, and vineyards in all their splendor were exactly what Jesus' eyes laid on when the prince of this world displayed all its glories and riches to Him. The price was much steeper than the mountain they stood on. Jesus referred back to God's Word in the Old Testament one final time and passed the third temptation. "Be gone, Satan! For it is written, 'You shall worship the Lord your God and Him only shall you serve.' Then the devil left Him, and behold, angels came and were ministering to Him" (Matthew 4:10–11).

Jesus enjoyed a rare moment of relieved elation while being attended to by angels. This relief was the brief spoils of a battle won, but Jesus knew full well the war was not nearly finished. "And when the devil had ended every temptation, he departed from Him until an opportune time" (Luke 4:13). Jesus would need some companions.

ALLIES

Author J. R. R. Tolkien masterfully introduces an assemblage of unforgettable adventurers in his classic tale *The Lord of the Rings*. Frodo and his three hobbit companions, Sam, Merry, and Pippin, are guided by Gandalf the wise wizard. Slowly, they meet and join forces with Gimli, an axe-wielding dwarf; Legolas, the elven archer; battle-ready Boromir; and the mysteriously charismatic ranger, Strider. Their diverse interplay, teamwork, and resourcefulness combine with threaded Christian themes of good versus evil, death and immortality, and the danger of power, through their travails. Together they form the fellowship of the ring and embark on a grand adventure like few have ever imagined.

Heroes often make alliances and for a variety of purposes. Primarily, those who come together seek a common goal. United forces make for good camaraderie, morale of the spirit, and exchange of ideas. Allies of a hero bring different skills to the group and can come from the most unlikely of places. Allies can help on a quest as well as inhibit it at times. Occasionally, there may even be a sketchy, shapeshifting type of character, who at first appears as a noble ally only to reveal himself later to be the opposite.

Soon after Jesus victoriously concluded His season of temptation, He sought students. His ministry was about to begin.

> And He went up on the mountain and called to Him those whom He desired, and they came to Him. And He appointed twelve (whom He also named apostles) so that they might be with Him and He might send them out to preach and have authority to cast out demons. He appointed the twelve: Simon (to whom He gave the name Peter); James the son of Zebedee and John the brother of James (to whom He gave the name Boanerges, that is, Sons of Thunder); Andrew, and Philip, and Bartholomew, and Matthew, and Thomas, and James the son of Alphaeus, and Thaddaeus, and Simon the Zealot, and Judas Iscariot, who betrayed Him. (MARK 3:13–19)

Not all the backgrounds of the twelve disciples of Christ are known. Their core was made up of fishermen, and among other personalities, a tax collector and a political zealot rounded out their eclectic company. Jesus called the twelve disciples with apparent significance. It underscored the twelve tribes of God's chosen people, the Israelites, in the Old Testament. Also, He played on the act of transitioning fishermen into fishers of men (Matthew 4:19).

Something new had begun. Although, when one considers the complete selection in retrospect, something seems amiss. A critical eye might suggest an omniscient God-man might have chosen better, particularly in one case. Yet Jesus was savvy all along. "Did I not choose you, the twelve? And yet one of you is a devil" (John 6:70). Regardless, this was the chosen fellowship of the King.

Not all the disciples are readily remembered, though certain names stand out more prominently than others. Jesus had an inner circle of three. On several occasions, Jesus drew Peter, James, and John closer for an exclusive teaching: when He raised Jairus's daughter from the dead, on the Mount of Transfiguration, and in the Garden of Gethsemane. Jesus routinely selected those three with intentionality and chose to reveal certain events, truths, and teachings to them, preparing them as the future leadership of His Church.

Specifically, Jesus referred to Simon Peter as the Rock. "And I tell you, you are Peter, and on this rock I will build My church, and the gates of hell shall not prevail against it" (Matthew 16:18). Peter would in time confess Jesus Christ as Lord, deny Him three times, and be reinstated by Jesus. This was a painful long-game lesson in faith and forgiveness for any future disciples of Christ to ponder.

James and John got nicknamed the "Sons of Thunder," presumably for their bold nature. On one occasion when Jesus was not received well in a town, James and John took trigger-ready issue.

> "Lord, do You want us to tell fire to come down from heaven and consume them?" But He turned and rebuked them. And they went on to another village. (LUKE 9:54–56)

On another occasion, they brazenly inquired about flanking Jesus' right and left when He entered His kingdom. The other ten disciples were less than thrilled with their presumption, and Jesus corrected them.

> To sit at My right hand or at My left is not Mine to grant, but it is for those for whom it has been prepared. (MARK 10:40)

Thomas bears the unfortunate moniker as "the Doubter." He demanded proof of Christ's identity, in conjunction with the exclusively divine act of resurrection from the dead. Jesus satisfied Thomas's concern by inviting him to touch His pierced hands and side. Thomas had to know for sure, and he received his answer, but not without one last powerful lesson from Jesus, tailored solely for him. "Jesus said to him, 'Have you believed because you have seen Me? Blessed are those who have not seen and yet have believed'" (John 20:29). While "Doubting Thomas" doesn't have the ring to it any disciple of Christ would desire, it is infinitely better than that of another disciple in their midst.

The name *Judas* will never be a popular choice in the maternity ward. The old adage "Keep your friends close and your enemies closer" could never have been truer. Jesus predicted that one of His disciples would betray Him (John 13:21), and so it happened:

> Then one of the twelve, whose name was Judas Iscariot, went to the chief priests and said, "What will you give me if I deliver Him over to you?" And they paid him thirty pieces of silver. And from that moment he sought an opportunity to betray Him. (MATTHEW 26:14–16)

Judas Iscariot was once an ally, but he would be remembered forever as an adversary, for the devil worked through him as he does all adversaries of God. The apostle Paul would later write, "For such men are false apostles, deceitful workmen, disguising themselves as apostles of Christ. And no wonder, for even Satan disguises himself as an angel of light" (2 Corinthians 11:13–14).

ADVERSARIES

Jesus had to contend with various villains through the course of His ministry. Demoniacs, scribes, Pharisees, and Sadducees regularly engaged Him in cloak-and-dagger dialogue. His only weapon was the Word of God. Once, while Jesus taught in the synagogue, He was approached by a demon-possessed naysayer.

> "Ha! What have You to do with us, Jesus of Nazareth? Have You come to destroy us? I know who You are—the Holy One of God." But Jesus rebuked him, saying, "Be silent and come out of him!" And when the demon had thrown him down in their midst, he came out of him, having done him no harm. And they were all amazed and said to one another, "What is this word? For with authority and power He commands the unclean spirits, and they come out!" (LUKE 4:34–36)

The Bible often presents the scribes, Pharisees, and Sadducees together, though each faction possessed different devious interests. The scribes mainly recopied the Scriptures. They focused on miniscule details to the very letter of the law and evolved into judgmental teachers. The Pharisees and Sadducees were both distinct religious political parties. They despised each other, yet they shared a common enemy in Jesus.

This triple threat of the scribes, Pharisees, and Sadducees took turns attempting to ridicule Jesus publicly. Their favorite game was entrapment through logical debates in the hope of exposing Him in front of the crowds as a false teacher. They questioned His authority, demanded He perform signs, and even accused Jesus of having a demon. Jesus navigated each instance with breathtaking unparalleled wisdom.

> But when the Pharisees heard that He had silenced the Sadducees, they gathered together. And one of them, a lawyer, asked Him a question to test Him. "Teacher, which is the great commandment in the Law?" And He said to him, "You shall love the Lord your God with all your heart and with all your soul and with all your mind. This is the great and first commandment. And a second is like it: You shall love your neighbor as yourself. On these two commandments depend all the Law and the Prophets." (MATTHEW 22:34-40)

Jesus frequently pointed out their sin through parables, and He routinely called them out for being hypocrites, blind guides, whitewashed tombs, and a brood of vipers. Some of them were so vexed they even attempted to stone Him. Jesus eventually flipped the tables on all of them by asking a question of His own.

> But He said to them, "How can they say that the Christ is David's son? For David himself says in the Book of Psalms, 'The Lord said to my Lord, "Sit at My right hand, until I make Your enemies Your footstool." ' David thus calls Him Lord, so how is He his son?" And in the hearing of all the people He said to His disciples, "Beware of the scribes, who like to walk

around in long robes, and love greetings in the marketplaces and the best seats in the synagogues and the places of honor at feasts, who devour widows' houses and for a pretense make long prayers. They will receive the greater condemnation." (Luke 20:41–47)

Jesus silenced them permanently that day. They didn't answer. The apparent best scholars of the day could not see the solution standing in front of them and were trapped in their own words. The sole remedy to the riddle was that the Messiah's Father would have to be God, but somehow also human from the lineage of David. They could not see and would never admit that Jesus was both in the flesh.

All they could do was plot to kill Him. Satan, the puppet master of sin, could not have been more pleased. Sin coursed through their veins, and all humankind's. No one would be free from culpability when it was time for Jesus' execution.

> Though devils all the world should fill,
>   All eager to devour us,
> We tremble not, we fear no ill;
>   They shall not overpow'r us.
> This world's prince may still
> Scowl fierce as he will,
>   He can harm us none.
>   He's judged; the deed is done;
> One little word can fell him.[25]

---

25   "A Mighty Fortress Is Our God," *LSB* 656:3.

A NECESSARY HORROR

See, My betrayer is at hand.

—MATTHEW 26:46

He had to keep a low profile, going incognito. The Nazi army surrounded his friends on all sides. It was not easy in the hot desert climate, but he kept digging. He knew something the Nazis didn't. At nightfall, thunder and lightning cracked as they uncovered the seal to the dark, cavernous tomb. The entrance cap slid open, and they peered down into the Well of Souls. Indiana Jones was about to face his biggest fears. He dropped a torch down to the bottom. Across the floor slithered thousands of snakes, his crippling kryptonite. The situation could not have been more uncomfortable. Yet it was a necessary horror for the ultimate prize—the ark of the covenant. The heroes of *Raiders of the Lost Ark* knew they must descend down into the danger by rope. Indy fired an unforgettable glance when his friend pointed out the snakes and told him to go first.

THE INMOST CAVE

When a hero approaches the inmost cave, it is occasionally literal, but usually it is metaphorical. He is about to face his greatest test. It is the point of no return. The narrative has been building for some time. Everything cared about has come to a head. Nothing comes easy as layers of horrors compound the situation. Sometimes it is an actual cave-like scenario with inevitable hidden hazards. Sometimes it is an interaction with others, representative of finally addressing the inner dread that haunts the hero. Regardless of the circumstances, truth is exacted in a defining moment of character identity.

Jesus' time on earth eventually came to a turning point. His Galilean ministry transitioned into a journey toward Jerusalem. "When the days drew near for Him to be taken up, He set His face to go to Jerusalem" (Luke 9:51). An imminent appointment awaited Him, and He knew it. His eventual march to Calvary was the only way to save the world. He would not waver; He could not break. Success was the lone option to defeat sin, death, and the power of the devil, winning forgiveness of sins and everlasting life for all who might believe. In perfect, intense obedience, Jesus set His face toward Jerusalem.

> The next day the large crowd that had come to the feast heard that Jesus was coming to Jerusalem. So they took branches of palm trees and went out to meet Him, crying out, "Hosanna! Blessed is He who comes in the name of the Lord, even the King of Israel!" And Jesus found a young donkey and sat on it, just as it is written, "Fear not, daughter of Zion; behold, your King is coming, sitting on a donkey's colt!" His disciples did not understand these things at first, but when Jesus was glorified, then they remembered that these things had been written about Him and had been done to Him. (JOHN 12:12–16)

Jesus' triumphant entry into Jerusalem is forever remembered as Palm Sunday. No gleaming white steed was used. The divinely human hero humbly rode in—on a donkey. Christ's great undertaking had begun. His arrival was greeted with fanfare from the crowd, yet plenty of danger lurked in hiding. As Jesus steered through the gauntlet of masses, sniper-ready scribes targeted their best plans for attack. Nevertheless, Jesus pressed onward. He had a big week ahead.

Passover was looming ominously. Logistical arrangements for the group needed to be made as well as meal preparations for the high holy day. An unblemished sacrificial lamb, of particular importance, needed to be acquired—a biblical foreshadowing of the greatest kind. God had a different Lamb in mind, and for a greater feast to come. Perhaps John the Baptist's words came to mind as Jesus strolled through the streets of Jerusalem early in the week. "Behold, the Lamb of God, who takes away the sin of the world" (John 1:29).

As Jesus went about His tasks, the paparazzi-like Pharisees riddled Him with questions. Their diabolical logic queries were designed to trap Jesus in His words. They sought condemning sound bites to spread hastily through their gossip network. A primitive form of social media to be sure, but no less damaging. Jesus made swift work of their best efforts. Their challenges were mere child's play for Him. "For the wisdom of this world is folly with God. For it is written, 'He catches the wise in their craftiness'" (1 Corinthians 3:19). The impromptu debates Jesus won paled in comparison to the many sufferings He would soon endure.

Jesus soon shared the Passover meal with His disciples, but with a twist. It was His Last Supper, and a final teaching, as well as a final prediction, was in order. In the soft, somber twilight of the evening, Jesus articulated a new type of meal born out of the Exodus celebration. His very body and blood would be the main course, imparting the forgiveness of sins (Matthew 26:26–29). Profound words to ponder for generations to come. That food for thought only weighed briefly on the disciples, Peter in particular. Christ's final forecast to them was imminent.

THE HERO STANDS ALONE

Jesus had shocked them earlier in the evening by saying one of them would betray Him. He shook them all the more when He led them out to the Garden of Gethsemane:

> "You will all fall away, for it is written, 'I will strike the shepherd, and the sheep will be scattered.' But after I am raised up, I will go before you to Galilee." Peter said to Him, "Even though they all fall away, I will not." And Jesus said to him, "Truly, I tell you, this very night, before the rooster crows twice, you will deny Me three times." (MARK 14:27–30)

Peter's noble naivete made him likeable enough. Yet his thin veneer of faith, impulsivity, and brash argumentative nature often set him up to learn painful lessons. This episode was no different. It served as a brief cue to Jesus that His band of allies, even His closest circle, was incredibly fragile at this point. They would be departing His company soon. Jesus would have to continue His journey alone.

Christ's ensemble cast of disciples, including the traitor, all played their parts in classic story form. Judas should not be mistaken for an antihero or a victim. His persona was more of the shapeshifter variety. The shapeshifter persona in the hero's journey pattern is a duplicitous one; this one seems trustworthy early on, but in the end he reveals a darker identity and motivations.

> While [Jesus] was still speaking, Judas came, one of the twelve, and with him a crowd with swords and clubs, from the chief priests and the scribes and the elders. Now the betrayer had given them a sign, saying, "The one I will kiss is the man. Seize Him and lead Him away under guard." (MARK 14:43–44)

The party was officially over. The disciples' celebratory evening came to an abrupt end. Judas's killjoy action changed the mood with greater magnitude than he could have possibly fathomed. The kiss of betrayal sealed their fate. Jesus declared that if the posse was looking for Him, they should let His disciples go. It was His last act of freedom. The disciples fled posthaste from the sword-drawn soldiers. Jesus went peacefully without a fight. He knew the necessary horror that awaited Him. He was taken into custody and brought to the belly of the beast—the Sanhedrin.

Christ's heroically dark cave-like experience transpired in the darkened courtyards of the palatial homes of Annas and Caiaphas. Annas, the former high priest of the Sanhedrin, and his son-in-law, Caiaphas, the acting high priest, presumably shared opposite ends of a courtyard. An unofficial gathering of the Sanhedrin came together. Under a tent of darkness, clandestine hearings took place by torchlight and would continue throughout the night.

Caiaphas and all the priests, elders, and scribes knew a consensus had to be reached swiftly. A long, drawn-out trial during the day would have riled up Jesus' enthusiastic fan base and potentially foiled the execution of their plans. An expedient hearing and charge were needed at night for an official Sanhedrin vote to be ratified first thing in the morning. The swift timing would build on their momentum and safeguard from any potential undoing. They had a tomb-like cave in mind for Jesus.

THE MOMENT(S) OF TRUTH

When Jesus arrived, they pounced on Him with accusations. None of the statements were true or consistent with corroborating witnesses. Then Caiaphas forced the issue of Jesus' true identity:

> And the high priest stood up in the midst and asked Jesus, "Have you no answer to make? What is it that these men testify against You?" But He remained silent and made no answer. Again the high priest asked Him, "Are You the Christ, the Son of the Blessed?" And Jesus said, "I am, and you will see the Son of Man seated at the right hand of Power, and coming with the clouds of heaven." And the high priest tore his garments and said, "What further witnesses do we need?

> You have heard His blasphemy. What is your decision?" And
> they all condemned Him as deserving death. (MARK 14:60–64)

The long night to remember devolved further into the morning hours of the morrow. The dawn rays of light brought forth no hope. The Sanhedrin council voted unanimously, save the likely abstention of two presumably secret followers of Christ, Joseph of Arimathea and Nicodemus. The verdict: death! Afterward, a pathetic game of political volleyball developed. Within a relatively short period of time, Jesus was tossed like a hot potato from Caiaphas and the Sanhedrin to Pontius Pilate, the Roman governor, to King Herod, and ultimately back to Pilate. All were culpable, but none wanted the blood on their hands.

The greatest reversal in the world occurred when blame finally rested on Jesus. Still, Pontius Pilate, far from innocent, tried his best to discern the truth. He even had a conversation with Jesus about it:

> Then Pilate said to Him, "So You are a king?" Jesus answered,
> "You say that I am a king. For this purpose I was born and for
> this purpose I have come into the world—to bear witness to
> the truth. Everyone who is of the truth listens to My voice."
> Pilate said to Him, "What is truth?" After he had said this, he
> went back outside to the Jews and told them, "I find no guilt
> in Him. But you have a custom that I should release one man
> for you at the Passover. So do you want me to release to you
> the King of the Jews?" They cried out again, "Not this man,
> but Barabbas!" Now Barabbas was a robber. (JOHN 18:37–40)

The bloodthirsty throng wanted death for Jesus. No compromise would do, but there was one caveat. They desired their religious laws be enforced under the jurisdiction of the Roman legal system, thus allowing them to stay protected in self-perceived innocence. Pontius Pilate saw he was losing the crowd as they grew more riotous. Pilate had much more to lose in his career than to gain by defending Jesus. And so it was that the one with the most authority to put an end to the whole sham of a trial shirked his responsibility.

So when Pilate saw that he was gaining nothing, but rather
that a riot was beginning, he took water and washed his
hands before the crowd, saying, "I am innocent of this man's
blood; see to it yourselves." And all the people answered,
"His blood be on us and on our children!" Then he released
for them Barabbas, and having scourged Jesus, delivered
Him to be crucified. (MATTHEW 27:24–26)

The truth is that everyone that has ever lived is responsible for Christ
being sentenced to death. The truth is that no one is innocent of sin save
Jesus. The truth stood before Pilate, but he could not see truth staring
him back in the face.

> Ride on, ride on in majesty!
> In lowly pomp ride on to die.
> O Christ, Thy triumphs now begin
> O'er captive death and conquered sin.
>
> Ride on, ride on in majesty!
> The angel armies of the sky
> Look down with sad and wond'ring eyes
> To see the approaching sacrifice.[26]

---

26   "Ride On, Ride On in Majesty," *LSB* 441:2–3.

CHAPTER

8

ENDURING
THE CURSE

*He shall bruise your head, and
you shall bruise His heel.*

—GENESIS 3:15

He was a formidable force. All the Achaean warriors attested he was the best of their extensive tribe. It was hard to disagree as his two magnificent horses, Dappled and Blonde, pulled him swiftly by chariot through the ranks of soldiers. His exquisite armor, gifted by Hephaestus himself, glistened in the sun on the Trojan beachhead. The mighty Achilles, the greatest champion the Greeks had ever known, was born of goddess and man. An ill-omened prophecy, however, hung over his head—should he go to battle, he would undoubtedly win glory, but surely die young.

His mother, Thetis, a sea nymph, sought to protect him from an early age. She dipped him as an infant in the river Styx, magically making him virtually invulnerable, save his heel by which she clutched him. When he was a young boy, she put him in hiding. Achilles, the champion warrior that he was, could not fight off his own compelling nature to enter battle. He eventually joined his Greek compatriots in war and led them valiantly.

The Trojan War, a laborious ordeal of ten years, mercifully neared its end. Homer's epic poem, the *Iliad*, nears its end with Achilles celebrating over his slain rival, Hector, while still enjoying his glorious day in the hot sun.

THE ORDEAL

The great ordeal for any hero is, by definition, never easy. It is the most harrowing of all confrontations. Everything the hero has trained for, learned, and studied gets put into action. No more practice; now it is for real. Everything is on the line. The hero must draw upon every fiber of wits, skill, allegiance, and resource to find victory. It does not always work out the way anyone anticipates.

Jesus' day of epic battle in the sun played out quite differently. He did not enter into His kingdom of glory with the usual optics of success. His battle, though, was more valiant. "New wars too shall arise, and once again some great Achilles to some Troy be sent."[27] The ominous prophecies of Christ's death would begin their impacting inflictions as the day ran its course. One by one they came true.

It had already been a long morning before the heat of the day bore down on Jesus. In the wee hours of Good Friday morning, King Herod Antipas had questioned Him. His court mocked Jesus further by dressing Him in a faux kingly wardrobe. The ridicule intensified as Jesus stood in front of the very man to whom John the Baptist's head had been presented on a platter. Jesus did not provide Herod's palace court any extra entertainment. He held His tongue. "He was oppressed, and He was afflicted, yet He opened not His mouth; like a lamb that is led to the slaughter, and like a sheep that before its shearers is silent, so He opened not His mouth" (Isaiah 53:7).

They hauled Jesus back across town to Pilate for the rest of the mock trial. In Pilate's attempt to appease the blood-seeking mob, he had Jesus scourged. While whipping may inflict one stinging cord of leather upon the flesh, scourging was grotesquely different. Roman scourging employed

---

27   Virgil, Eclogue 4, *Great Books of the Western World: Virgil*, ed. Robert Maynard Hutchins (Chicago, IL: William Benton Publisher, Encyclopedia Brittanica, Inc, 1952), 15, line 36.

a multi-ended whip fashioned with small sharp projectile objects attached to the ends of the chords. It was designed to inflict as much physically punishing pain as possible. "I gave My back to those who strike, and My cheeks to those who pull out the beard; I hid not My face from disgrace and spitting" (Isaiah 50:6).

Jesus' back was mutilated by the end of the scourging. The soldiers stuck the royal robe with which they had mocked Him back upon His raw, bloody skin. That only whet the appetite of the crowd. They would not be satisfied until Jesus was dead. Shouts of "Crucify Him, crucify Him" erupted, and Pilate finally caved to their demands. "As many were astonished at you—His appearance was so marred, beyond human semblance, and His form beyond that of the children of mankind" (Isaiah 52:14).

The sadistic soldiers even constructed a makeshift kingly crown out of a vine of thorns and crammed it on His head. They appointed a large wooden cross to Jesus, and He began His "way of suffering"[28] from Pontius Pilate's tribunal to Golgotha, the Place of the Skull. The insults continued to rain down:

> And the soldiers led Him away inside the palace (that is, the governor's headquarters), and they called together the whole battalion. And they clothed Him in a purple cloak, and twisting together a crown of thorns, they put it on Him. And they began to salute Him, "Hail, King of the Jews!" And they were striking His head with a reed and spitting on Him and kneeling down in homage to Him. And when they had mocked Him, they stripped Him of the purple cloak and put His own clothes on Him. And they led Him out to crucify Him. (MARK 15:16–20)

The scourging, the heat, the early stages of dehydration, the weight of the cross's wood beam, the incline, the crown of thorns, the psychological torment—all these took their toll on Jesus' body. The steps of Christ

---

28   The *Via Dolorosa* beginning at the temple is the traditional path, though many historical scholars believe the route from Pilate's palace is much more plausible.

slowed to a halt in exhaustion. The soldiers swiftly called upon a passerby, Simon of Cyrene, to assist Jesus, and the pitiless parade continued. Once at Calvary, the soldiers stripped Jesus of any remaining dignity, exposing Him for all the world to see. Next, they took spikes and pounded them into the ends of His limbs. "For dogs encompass Me; a company of evildoers encircles Me; they have pierced My hands and feet—I can count all My bones—they stare and gloat over Me; they divide My garments among them, and for My clothing they cast lots" (Psalm 22:16–18).

As soon as Jesus was nailed to the tree, they raised Him up. No position of contortion could give comfort; no wiggle room gave relief. Not even a drop of moisture fell to soothe His mouth for a merciful moment. The soldiers offered Him a bitter herbal cocktail of wine mixed with gall, but as soon as Jesus tasted it, He refused. "They gave Me poison for food, and for My thirst they gave Me sour wine to drink" (Psalm 69:21).

At one point, a squabble broke out. A small sign reading the words "Jesus of Nazareth, the King of the Jews" was written by Pilate and positioned above Jesus on the cross (John 19:19). The Jewish contingency quickly grew annoyed, as the inscription was written in three different languages and evident to all. They believed it should have read, "This man said, I am King of the Jews" (v. 21). Pontius Pilate, done with capitulating to a hypercritical crowd, denied the request. The sign stayed as was written, thus stating the truth. Pilate's decision remains the best rejection of an author to his editors in the history of the world.

That day undoubtedly seemed as long as a thousand years, as Jesus hung on the cross. He waited to die, mangled, naked, and alone. It seemed as if even God the Father had turned His back on His only Son. From a vague distance, Jesus could see something. Jesus squinted through sweaty, bloody eyes and a swollen brow to see the forms of His mother, Mary, and a beloved disciple, John. "My friends and companions stand aloof from my plague, and my nearest kin stand far off" (Psalm 38:11).

How could it be that the only one without sin, the only perfect being, could be held responsible for all of humanity, even to death? "Indeed, under the law almost everything is purified with blood, and without the shedding of blood there is no forgiveness of sins" (Hebrews 9:22).

THE FATAL FLAW

As the legend goes in some of the later Roman epic poetry that augmented Homer's original Greek story, Achilles eventually met his downfall. One night, with Samson-like arrogance, Achilles shared his weakness to a girl he loved. Trojan archrival Paris, the brother of fallen Hector, overheard the information. Paris notched his archer's bow and immediately acted. The fateful arrow flew, aided by the god Apollo, and dripping with Murphy's Law,[29] it plunged into the heel of Achilles. The greatest of all Greek warriors died soon after. The fateful foretelling of his demise had come true.

The fatal flaw of a tragic hero is usually an issue diametrically opposed to the more prominent qualities of the hero. Often, the flaw is obvious to those around the hero: for example, an addiction, or a lack of character in a certain area of their personality. It thwarts the hero from succeeding; for example, the lack of ability of a brilliant physician who cannot heal himself, the endless greed of a wealthy lord, or the hubris of a king. For Achilles, the ridiculous event of the mightiest warrior's own undoing through a wound to the heel is unfathomable. "And so the famous Achilles, after triumphing over such great heroes, was defeated by a coward who had stolen away from Greece another man's wife."[30]

As for Jesus, it is an absolutely absurd juxtaposition that the only one in the world without sin was to be punished for sin. It is inconceivable, and yet so it was foretold. Christ, who had no sin, who knew no sin, actually became sin. This fact proved to be fatal. "Therefore I will divide Him a portion with the many, and He shall divide the spoil with the strong, because He poured out His soul to death and was numbered with the transgressors; yet He bore the sin of many, and makes intercession for the transgressors" (Isaiah 53:12).

---

29   Murphy's Law states the timeless adage "If anything can go wrong, it will go wrong."

30   Ovid, *The Metamorphoses of Ovid*, Book 12, translated by Mary M. Innes (London: Penguin Books, 1955), 284.

It is imperative to know Jesus did not actually commit sin, but rather He became sin personified. How might this be properly understood? The sin of the world was transferred to Him. God had established this practice and set it up long before. In the Old Testament, Moses and Aaron were instructed by God to lead the Israelites through an annual religious practice. The tenth day of the seventh month was Yom Kippur, the Day of Atonement. Two goats and a male sheep were among the sacrificial animals. The high priest would cast lots over the goats. One would be the sin offering for the people, and the other would serve as the scapegoat, sent out to wander in the wilderness. The sins of the community were transferred to the scapegoat, which carried those sins out away from their midst.

Meanwhile, the male sheep was also sacrificed as a burnt offering to make atonement for the people. Jesus would later fulfill this concept in a multifaceted way. Christ serves in dual capacity as a stand-in for both the scapegoat and the unblemished sheep. The sin of the world bore down upon Him as He carried the cross outside of the city walls. And He is the sinless, unblemished Lamb of God who takes away the sins of the world. Christ atones for the sins of the world so that we might be saved. "For our sake He made Him to be sin who knew no sin, so that in Him we might become the righteousness of God" (2 Corinthians 5:21).

The ancient prophecies of the crucifixion continued to ring true. The incongruous nature of Jesus, bleeding His holy, precious, innocent blood for the sins of the world, could not have been more heartbreaking. This Passion paradox continued to play right into the pierced hands of Christ crucified.

It is quite conceivable that the devil cackled with delight throughout the excruciating process of the crucifixion. Little did Satan realize he was cheering for his own defeat. "I will put enmity between you and the woman, and between your offspring and her offspring; He shall bruise your head, and you shall bruise His heel" (Genesis 3:15).

As Satan sank his fangs into Jesus' heel, the world was in the process of being healed. "But He was pierced for our transgressions; He was crushed for our iniquities; upon Him was the chastisement that brought us peace, and with His wounds we are healed" (Isaiah 53:5). And in His death, Christ stomped His heel, crushing the serpent's head instantly.

> Stricken, smitten, and afflicted,
>> See Him dying on the tree!
> 'Tis the Christ, by man rejected;
>> Yes, my soul, 'tis He, 'tis He!
> 'Tis the long-expected Prophet,
>> David's Son, yet David's Lord;
> Proofs I see sufficient of it:
>> 'Tis the true and faithful Word.[31]

---

31   "Stricken, Smitten, and Afflicted," *LSB* 451:1.

A Marvelous Godsend

*Father, forgive them for they
know not what they do.*

—LUKE 23:34

R ejoicing on the anchorage shoreline quickly swelled into festive
revelry continuing well into the night. All the warships in the enemy
fleet had sailed away. The grisly ten-year war was over. It was time to
celebrate. The citizens of Troy, though, had a much wilder evening ahead
than any suspected. Unbeknownst to them, one Greek vessel hadn't left.
It had been repurposed into a large wooden horse. A stranded beachhead
messenger suggested it was an offering to the goddess Athena. The Trojans
couldn't resist bringing the monumental equine inside their impregnable
citadel for the merrymaking. After all, with the gods smiling, it would
surely confirm their impervious nature. This was exactly what Odysseus
wanted the Trojans to think.

Odysseus, the most cunning of all Greek soldiers, schemed a ploy
so ingenious that no one saw it coming. He and several of his men hid
silently inside the dark, ark-like wooden horse they had built, waiting for
the best moment to strike. The stratagem was perfect. Even as the Trojans'

winecups were full to the brim with intoxicating pride, the Greeks were busy sailing right back toward them. Odysseus, clad in fallen Achilles' armor, stealthily slipped out of the wooden womb of the horse. He and his men unlocked the city gates. Just when the Trojans thought the war over and won, and the Greek spirit to fight dead, an unprecedented maneuver altered their fate forever. New life sprang forth with vim. Odysseus, aided by Athena, led the Greeks in to sack Troy for good. This was epic subterfuge at its finest.

THE ULTIMATE BOON

The ultimate boon is the triumphing conquest of the hero. It is typically understood as the *seizing of the sword* moment. The goal of the hero's quest culminates as the prize is finally grasped in hand. The more unpredictable the victory, the more satisfying the story. If there is a surprise twist, a third-act-turn so shocking no one expects it, then all the better. The hero surfaces from combat with a reward, be it success, the realization of truth, a loved one, or an artifact of tremendous significance. The hero has achieved his ultimate objective, although he might not be completely free from danger. The journey is not complete, not quite yet.

Jesus looked far from triumphant in His final moments hanging on the cross. The devil most likely crowed with self-satisfaction, waiting to count down the clock until the Lord of Life was dead. Yet how could Satan actually think he could cross swords with God and defeat Him? It must have been blind pride. After Satan fell "like lightning from heaven" (Luke 10:18), he most likely could not see true reality through his demonic delusions of grandeur. He was hell-bent on dethroning God to begin with, and he never ceased striving to usurp His authority thereafter.

As crafty as the devil thought he was, God is infinitely more clever. Other than Jesus, not a soul could see what was coming, not even Lucifer. Jesus even spelled it out for the people plainly while extended on the cross. "Father, forgive them, for they know not what they do" (Luke 23:34).

Satan's mind, depraved as it is, would have done well to recall what Jesus had said earlier that week, "Now is the judgment of this world; now will the ruler of this world be cast out" (John 12:31), or even the very previous evening, "The ruler of this world is judged" (John 16:11). Yet just when Satan was about to take the throne of God for himself, God turned the tables on him. The devil was destined to fail.

The devil had continued his streak of working temptation and sin through humanity, full throttle, from Adam and Eve, to Peter ("Get behind Me, Satan!" [Matthew 16:23]), to Judas ("Then Satan entered into Judas called Iscariot, who was of the number of the twelve" [Luke 22:3]). The prince of darkness was quite content watching the manifestation of sin lead the people of the world toward eternal condemnation, death, and hell.

The great cosmic dilemma that had lingered since the fall of humankind in the Garden of Eden persisted. Humankind sinned; therefore, humankind must die. Every soul remained culpable on an individual basis. Inconceivable to all, God (who alone can forgive) in His justice solved this cosmic dilemma by becoming man (who can die) and heroically suffering as a sacrifice for all of humankind's sins.

The Word had become flesh. Jesus is 100 percent God and 100 percent man at the same time. This hypostatic union[32] accomplished vicarious atonement for the sins of the world. Keep in mind that just because Jesus is all God doesn't mean He could bear suffering through physical pain any more easily than we could, because He is all man too.

Though Jesus had the opportunity to take full advantage of His divine nature and come down from the cross, He chose instead to bear the sins of the world on the cross.

> And those who passed by derided Him, wagging their heads and saying, "Aha! You who would destroy the temple and rebuild it in three days, save Yourself, and come down from the cross!" So also the chief priests with the scribes mocked

---

32   The personal union of Christ. "There are two natures, the divine and the human, in the incarnate Christ. Scripture expressly teaches that these two natures do not subsist by themselves, but that they have been united in to the one person of the Logos" (see Galatians 4:4). Martin Chemnitz, *The Two Natures in Christ*, translated by J. A. O. Preus (St. Louis, MO: Concordia Publishing House, 1971), 15.

Him to one another, saying, "He saved others; He cannot save Himself." (MARK 15:29–31)

Once again, Jesus resisted temptation and continued to pay for the sins of the world in the process.

As Jesus breathed His last breaths, the devil had Jesus right where he wanted Him—or so he thought. The greatest comeback victory ever was about to go down. Just as sin entered the world through one man, Adam, eternal grace was about to enter the world through the Second Adam, Jesus.

> Yet death reigned from Adam to Moses, even over those whose sinning was not like the transgression of Adam, who was a type of the one who was to come. But the free gift is not like the trespass. For if many died through one man's trespass, much more have the grace of God and the free gift by the grace of that one man Jesus Christ abounded for many. (ROMANS 5:14–15)

ATONEMENT WITH THE FATHER

Ironically, the phrase "atonement with the father" is used frequently for this stage of the hero's journey. The source of the innate yearning a child has for reconciliation with the father could not be clearer. Jesus substitutes and serves as the profound cure-all for this delicate relational dynamic.

> For God so loved the world, that He gave His only Son, that whoever believes in Him should not perish but have eternal life. For God did not send His Son into the world to condemn the world, but in order that the world might be saved through Him. (JOHN 3:16–17)

The wrath of God the Father bore down completely and emphatically upon Jesus that day at Calvary's mount. God the Father exacted His penalty of death, and Jesus absorbed the full brunt of the blow. Jesus, suffering physical despair in the moment, cried out, "My God, My God, why have You forsaken Me?" (Matthew 27:46).

In agonizing bodily shifts that granted no reprieve of pain, He sipped the bitter-tasting cup of death. "When Jesus had received the sour wine, He said, 'It is finished,' and He bowed His head and gave up His spirit" (John 19:30). Jesus, the unblemished Lamb of God, breathed His last with one final word from the cross. "Then Jesus, calling out with a loud voice, said, 'Father, into Your hands I commit My spirit!' And having said this He breathed His last" (Luke 23:46).

Sheer darkness blanketed the sky. An earthquake rumbled the ground underfoot. News spread quickly that the temple curtain ripped in half. All the while, Christ had the presence of mind to utter His powerful words from the cross, one after the other. So powerful was the scene that a Roman centurion exclaimed, "Truly this man was the Son of God!" (Mark 15:39).

Jesus died and entered into His reign of glory. God the Father was satisfied, for the sins of the world were paid for with Christ's holy, precious, and innocent blood. John, likely the youngest disciple, watched from a distance with Jesus' mother, Mary. John would later write of what he had witnessed. "He is the propitiation [atonement] for our sins, and not for ours only but also for the sins of the whole world" (1 John 2:2). Through His death, Christ Jesus seized the reward, and humanity's sins are forgiven forever.

JUSTIFICATION

Jesus served as the perfect sacrifice. He made it just as if sinners had no sin. He justified the world before God the Father. Just as Moses led the Israelites from bondage in Egypt to the Promised Land, Jesus freed humanity from the slavery of sin. The way to the promised land of eternal forgiveness was for Him to go through the cross in death. And with that brilliant move, God flipped the tables on the devil forever. It was Jesus' ultimate boon.

What happened next was unprecedented grace that still extends to God's people today through the sacred meal of Holy Communion. God had established the Passover meal with the Israelites in Egyptian bondage, well over a millennium prior. God directed them specifically with the unblemished Passover lamb, "You shall not break any of its bones" (Exodus 12:46). The psalmist also prophesied about the Messiah to come, "He keeps all His bones; not one of them is broken" (Psalm 34:20). These two verses are fascinating to keep in mind: when the Roman soldiers came by to guarantee Jesus' death, they "broke the legs of the first, and of the other who had been crucified with Him. But when they came to Jesus and saw that He was already dead, they did not break His legs" (John 19:32–33).

God continued to weave a thread of His unpredictable grace through all human history. John later concluded his observations, "For these things took place that the Scripture might be fulfilled: 'Not one of His bones will be broken'" (John 19:36). All these links are significant in the chain of God's forgiveness, which culminates in the Lord's Supper, through which believers partake of the body and blood of Christ—the Lamb of God who takes away the sin of the world.

Soon after Jesus' death, Joseph of Arimathea and Nicodemus, two of Jesus' secret disciples in the Sanhedrin, went to Pontius Pilate. Joseph boldly asked if they could remove Jesus' body, for there was a nearby garden with a tomb in which no one had been laid. Pilate agreed. Joseph and Nicodemus carefully took Jesus' lifeless body down and gently prepared it with spices and aloes. They wrapped Him in fine linen as the Jewish custom called for, and they laid Him to rest.

Good Friday had mercifully concluded. Satan had been vanquished. Jesus had paid the ultimate sacrifice. The people of the earth were saved. Years later, the apostle Peter summed up the amazing turn of events: "He Himself bore our sins in His body on the tree, that we might die to sin and live to righteousness. By His wounds you have been healed" (1 Peter 2:24).

However sweet victory's reward is, climatic triumph usually beckons the hero homeward to his ordinary world. The hero must cast festivities away and prepare for the return trip of his journey. After the Trojan horse and the defeat of Troy, Odysseus still had an entire odyssey ahead of him on his road back home to Greece and his family.

Jesus' redemptive work was complete, but something still remained for Him to do, like a purchased gift waiting to be wrapped. As meaningful as His death was, He would not remain dead. While Christ's death paid for the sins of the world, He would rise and live to apply it. He would bring "life and immortality to light" (2 Timothy 1:10). He would provide a living hope of legacy for all to come after. Christ would continue His journey of justification as He rested in the tomb. Meanwhile, a long Saturday loomed.

> What Thou, my Lord, has suffered
>   Was all for sinners' gain;
> Mine, mine was the transgression,
>   But Thine the deadly pain.
> Lo, here I fall, my Savior!
>   'Tis I deserve Thy place;
> Look on me with Thy favor,
>   And grant to me Thy grace.[33]

---

33   "O Sacred Head, Now Wounded," *LSB* 450:3.

RETURN FROM THE ABYSS

He went and proclaimed to spirits in prison.

—1 PETER 3:19

The hero lay still in the cool chamber, seemingly lifeless. He had trained so hard and battled so valiantly, but the enemy's illegal kick to his previously injured leg wounded him severely. His dreams were dead. Daniel LaRusso could not continue competing in the All-Valley Karate Championship. He had just finished writhing in agonizing tears in front of a large crowd that included his mother and his girlfriend. He was going through the unique, humiliating hell only a high school student could imagine, steeped in physical pain and emotional shame. He had done great, fought his way into the final match, and proved his point— Daniel held his own against the black-belted Cobra Kai punks who kept tormenting him, but his opportunity for ultimate vindication was over. Daniel's loved ones filed out of the room one by one, offering the fallen hero a quiet moment of solace. Yet a return chance still glimmered for him. Daniel stopped his sensei, Mr. Miyagi, and attempted to convince him of one last possibility.

Daniel still sought balance. He used to have it back home in New Jersey, but ever since he moved to the upside-down world of Los Angeles, he'd been thrown off-kilter. If he could somehow find a way to stand his ground and face his enemy in the finals—win or lose—he would regain self-esteem and restore balance in his life. Mr. Miyagi taught Daniel many lessons, most importantly the necessity of balance. Daniel knew it, and so did Miyagi. With an understanding sigh and a powerful clap, Mr. Miyagi rubbed his hands together. His mystical Okinawan healing technique was risky, but it was the only momentary solution. Daniel gingerly limped his way from the locker room, down the hall, and out to the ring for one final shot at victory and inner peace. The match began intensely against defending champion Johnny Lawrence, his sworn enemy. Finally, one definitive point remained to decide the champion. The Karate Kid's road back to restoration was almost complete.

THE ROAD BACK

A desired return to the home of origin is inevitable for almost every hero. While the initial call to adventure inspired or reluctantly compelled the hero earlier, a similarly corresponding call beckons a return home. The pathway back is generally not free from danger. It often mirrors the perils of the quest from the beginning. The hero must return from his quest, but not empty-handed. Typically, one last accomplishment is required. The hero must vanquish an enemy in a great external struggle, and this is usually accompanied by an inner struggle as well. Only after dealing with these can the hero truly return home and complete the adventure.

Christ had been utterly humiliated. Technically, He had been in the state of humiliation for some time. Ever since the Word became flesh, God had been wrapped in humanity, the immortal shrouded in mortality, with all the aches and pains that come with it. To be exact, Jesus had been enduring humiliation for His entire earthly life. From His incarnation at His conception via the annunciation of Mary, to being laid to rest on the evening of Good Friday, Jesus suffered humiliation. The Apostles' Creed succinctly summarizes this state of humiliation and has been remembered and confessed for nearly two millennia: "[He] was conceived by the Holy Spirit, born of the virgin Mary, suffered under Pontius Pilate, was crucified, died, and was buried."[34]

Historical prophecies continued to ring true, right up to the details of Jesus' grave. Jesus' burial in the tomb of a rich man was amazingly foretold by the prophet Isaiah.

> By oppression and judgment He was taken away; and as for His generation, who considered that He was cut off out of the land of the living, stricken for the transgression of My people? And they made His grave with the wicked and with a rich man in His death, although He had done no violence, and there was no deceit in His mouth. (Isaiah 53:8–9)

Joseph of Arimathea was well off, and he took care of all of the logistics, as only wealthy society members can do.

> When it was evening, there came a rich man from Arimathea, named Joseph, who also was a disciple of Jesus. He went to Pilate and asked for the body of Jesus. [Jesus would otherwise have been buried among the criminals.] Then Pilate ordered it to be given to him. And Joseph took the body and wrapped it in a clean linen shroud and laid it in his own new tomb, which he had cut in the rock. And he rolled a great stone to the entrance of the tomb and went away. (Matthew 27:57–60)

Christ's salvific work on the cross defeated the devil. He destroyed sin, delivering forgiveness to the world via His innocent, sacrificial bloodshed. "He is the propitiation for our sins, and not for ours only but also for the sins of the whole world" (1 John 2:2). Yet one major dilemma lingered. Jesus was still dead. If Christ was to triumph over sin, death, and the power of the devil, one of those three foes remained.

---

34   Luther's Small Catechism, Second Article.

MAGIC FLIGHT

The road back for the hero is sometimes called the *magic flight*. The flight can break one of two ways for the hero. The hero may still be in imminent danger, even after victory. The prize of the quest may have been obtained, but an easy-going escape with said prize is a different story. The knight may have slain the mountain cave dragon, but the cave might very well collapse before he flees to safety. The end of the journey may sometimes require just as much courage as the beginning. Christ's road back was not like this, fleeing a victorious scene full of danger and suspense.

Some epics position the hero to succeed. If the hero is somehow safeguarded by the gods or protected by some supernatural aid, then the return trip of the hero may be relatively uneventful. Accordingly, this sequence is often omitted in modern storytelling for this reason. Christ's road back wasn't an inconsequential non-event though. Jesus was sent by God the Father. His quest was clearly commissioned by the Father. Jesus also is God, which suggests a gentle road back for Him after His victory. Our hero Jesus, though, is still dead at this point in His story. If anything is known about Jesus' *modus operandi*, a twist in the template narrative is afoot.

Jesus' body lay in the tomb, lifeless. He was dead in the flesh, unequivo-cally and without a doubt. The Roman soldier's spear that pierced His side laid claim to that fact. The water and blood that flowed from His side bespoke the truth: Jesus was dead. Jesus' state of humiliation was merci-fully ended. However, something miraculous occurred in the tomb. At a certain point, after Jesus was crucified, died, and was buried, He was made alive in the spirit. "For Christ also suffered once for sins, the righteous for the unrighteous, that He might bring us to God, being put to death in the flesh but made alive in the spirit" (1 Peter 3:18).

Jesus' death was similar to every other human death. He died, and His body was in the tomb, but where was His spirit at that point? Jesus is entirely God but also entirely human, up to and including a vital detail: Jesus has a soul. Jesus' soul is a soul like any other human possesses, albeit with the distinction that it is united to His divine nature. Jesus' dead body lay hollow in the tomb. Had a spiritual postmortem been done, it would have revealed Jesus was not locked in a soul-sleep but was in fact in His state of exaltation.

Christians believe that after death one is immediately with God in paradise. The comforting words of Jesus to the thief on the cross still comfort dying Christians to this day. "Truly, I say to you, today you will be with Me in paradise" (Luke 23:43). The believer's soul is transported to God's presence, while the body lies waiting for the Last Day, when Christ will return and the dead rise to life everlasting with resurrected bodies. Why should Jesus' soul be any different? He told us where His spirit was going from the cross. "Father, into Your hands I commit My spirit!" (Luke 23:46), not to mention the fact that He also just confirmed to the thief he would be with Him in paradise that day.

After Jesus was buried, the next clause in the Apostles' Creed gives an eerie pause to some: "He descended into hell." What was Jesus doing there? As incongruously backward as it sounds, Jesus' first act in His state of exaltation was His descent into hell. It was a presumably brief excursion, but it was a necessary step on His road back. In His state of exaltation, Jesus' physical presence verified Him to be the risen Messiah who conquered death, present in the very realm of the dead. Christ descended victorious over His creatures, the fallen angels and unbelieving human souls in hell. No realm, not even Sheol, would escape Christ's triumphant reign.

Jesus did not descend into hell to suffer. His suffering had concluded. He went there to proclaim victory over hell, the devil, and the unbelieving disobedient inhabitants from ages past. While this event may seem like some bizarre divine *schadenfreude*,[35] Christ's descent into hell served a very different purpose. Much like victors in battle will overrun their enemy's stronghold at the conclusion of war, Jesus invaded Satan's dominion. God, having defeated the devil, victoriously occupied the territory of the enemy. Jesus announced conquest as He preached to the spirits in prison.

---

35 A German word translated literally as "harm-joy," meaning the experience of pleasure, joy, or self-satisfaction that comes from learning of or witnessing the troubles, failures, or humiliation of another.

Lutherans historically extend their theology only as far as the Scriptures permit. The Scriptures mention very little about this extraordinary excursion of Christ. We would be wise not to speculate beyond what the Bible states clearly. Indeed, temptation leads many a person to contemplate the specific details of what happens to those poor souls in hell that are gone from this world. Ah, but for a brief moment . . .

ABANDON HOPE, ALL YE WHO ENTER HERE

Amusingly, one poetically gifted Christian theologian, Dante, did painstakingly venture to explore this cryptic episode of Jesus in hell. Dante wrote the *Inferno*, his vision of hell, as if entering it on Good Friday, AD 1300. He fictitiously inserted himself into his writing, choosing to be escorted by a literary hero of his, the Roman poet Virgil.[36] At one point, Virgil referenced Christ's descent into hell: "I beheld a puissant [powerful] one arrive Amongst us, with victorious trophy crown'd." Virgil then listed numerous patriarchs by name and many more of the Israelite faith that Christ saved from hell, "whom he to bliss Exalted."[37]

Unfortunately for Virgil, he apparently held no faith of a coming Messiah, as he had died before Christ was born. Thus, from Dante's Roman Catholic perspective, Virgil did not recognize the importance of Jesus' arrival. He only spoke generically of a powerful one who rescued the Hebrew forefathers of Christianity but left him behind in eternal hell. As Dante progressed through his *Divine Comedy*,[38] Virgil escorted him through purgatory but was not permitted into heaven.

This "Harrowing of Hell" episode regarding Christ's descent there is considered by some Catholics as Christ's mission of preaching to the

---

36 Virgil was commissioned by Caesar Augustus to produce an epic poem for Roman national identity. He succeeded in his masterpiece, the *Aeneid*, in which the hero, Aeneas, also experiences a trip through the underworld of Hades, escorted by Dido.

37 Dante Alighieri, *The Divine Comedy of Dante Alighieri: Hell, Purgatory, Paradise*, trans. Henry F. Cary, The Harvard Classics, ed. Charles W. Eliot, vol. 20 (New York: P. F. Collier and Son, 1909), Canto IV, 18.

38 Dante's *Divine Comedy* is a three-act epic poem following his vision through hell (*Inferno*), purgatory (*Purgatorio*), and heaven (*Paradiso*).

spirits in hell, and more importantly, freeing them from that fiery fate. While fun to entertain for a few fleeting seconds, we do well to remember that it is not biblical but rather theological fan fiction. In the *Inferno*, Dante famously penned the line, "Abandon hope, all ye who enter here," posted at the gates of hell. Dante's words, while iconic, do not apply to Jesus, who truly provides hope for all humankind via the Gospel.

The good news is that we need not wander through wonderings of sin, death, or hell while the devil points his finger in our face. Christ made the trip, walked "through the valley of the shadow of death" (Psalm 23:4), and dwelled there for us. "For this is why the gospel was preached even to those who are dead, that though judged in the flesh the way people are, they might live in the spirit the way God does" (1 Peter 4:6).

Jesus is the escorting companion for all believers through the gates of heaven. And the journey for the Christian is instantaneously swifter than Dante's musing. "For God so loved the world, that He gave His only Son, that whoever believes in Him should not perish but have eternal life" (John 3:16). In order for Christ to reconcile believers to Himself, something needed to be done. Christ would make forgiveness of sins not only believable but confessable as well. While Jesus died to pay for sins, He lives to apply forgiveness. In order for people to believe, He rose from the dead.

Christ descended into hell and preached to the spirits in prison, announcing the victory of God. That proclaimed truth still reverberates through the corridors of hell, and will for all eternity. Jesus' road back was all but complete, exaltation begun, and a rising Gospel message shared. Christ is the firstborn of the dead, and He would make it so for all believers who would come after Him. He would create a new reality from death to life, for Him and the world to come.

Jesus is the saving guide to heaven for all who believe in Him. Because of Him, there is no need to fear the underworld of hell, sin, death, or the power of the devil. The devil once tempted Jesus, quipping lines from Psalm 91:11–12 (see Matthew 4:5–7). It's no wonder the devil ended his quote there. As if in poetic justice, the very next line proved the ultimate point. "You will tread on the lion and the adder; the young lion and the serpent you will trample underfoot" (Psalm 91:13). Christ's heel had indeed crushed the head of the serpent, and He triumphed over all.

Heroes rise to the occasion. Daniel LaRusso stood on his one good leg, in the legendary crane-kick stance. His arms extended for balance, his heel poised and ready to strike the head of the cobra, or in his case, the Cobra Kai. At the referee's whistle, Daniel's outer struggle and inner struggle converged as he majestically kicked his opponent for the decisive win. Daniel, the Karate Kid, was triumphantly restored, in resurrection-like fashion, and his road back to balance was complete.

> Mighty Victim from the sky,
> Hell's fierce pow'rs beneath You lie;
> You have conquered in the fight,
> You have brought us life and light.
> Alleluia![39]

39 "At the Lamb's High Feast We Sing," *LSB* 633:5.

PHOENIX RISING

He is not here, for He has risen.

—MATTHEW 28:6

D eath. It is the definitive dilemma of humankind. Every person that walks the earth must come to terms with this reality. Who can beat it? Death is permanent. Humanity's dream quest of immortality, however, has always enjoyed widespread appeal throughout the history of the world. Humanity desperately desires everlasting life to be true. Humankind has yearned for it, consistently sought it out, and even attempted to invent it. It is embedded in our stories of hope.

The climactic peak of the hero's journey is when the hero experiences his most dire brush with death. This is the final confrontation, which if lost will result in the suffering of many. Ultimately, the hero must somehow prevail, cheat death, and escape. The great task of confronting death must be accomplished in a very meaningful way. Success represents not merely the hero's individual victory but also a restoration of other people and the greater community. A good story may resurrect the hero, but a great story will resurrect much more: hope, opportunity, and freedom. Characteristically, different types of death and resurrection sequences are employed for a hero: psychological, relational, communal, or even a spiritual death. Death is the end of the story, and there are no sequels.

It is exceedingly difficult to find any epic or modern hero who actually dies a physical death and also physically rises from the grave. There is almost always some weak, bail-out explanation that cheapens the actual physical death and resurrection of the hero. Many modern fanboys will cry foul at this notion, pointing to Superman's widely publicized death and return in the comics. The problem is that Superman didn't actually die. Unfortunately, we have to enter full-blown geek mode to understand this. Apologies in advance; ready?

It was 1992. Yours truly happened to be in the pinnacle of his comic book collecting days. The national news broke a massive, earth-shattering story, and consequently the media everywhere gave it a lot of attention. The DC Comics executives had cooked up an idea to revive sales: they were going to kill off Superman. Up to this point, occasionally a comic hero might die, but they would stay dead. It was an unwritten yet widely understood sacrosanct rule. While it seems silly now, it was a monumental deal, living through the moment in real time. One was not sure what the future looked like without the icon for truth, justice, and the American way flying around pop culture.

I faithfully bought my copy, which included a tombstone-looking cover, a death notice clipping from *The Daily Planet*, and an actual black armband with Superman's insignia on it, apparently to mourn his loss in the real world. All this was sealed in a black bag with a bleeding Superman logo.[40] No marketing expense was spared. It worked like a charm, and the DC Comics executives laughed all the way to the bank, achieving record global sales in volume and time.

Meanwhile, Doomsday, the aptly named and newly invented villain, had killed Superman in a battle royale the likes of which Metropolis had never seen. Only . . . Superman wasn't technically dead. One year later, during another highly successful marketing campaign for Superman's return, DC Comics revealed that he had been in a Kryptonian healing coma the whole time. Being an alien from another planet, it was quite understandable that he only seemed dead to residents of earth.

---

40   Yes, I still own a copy of *Superman #75* to this day.

Needless to say, the news was met with great dissatisfaction from the fan base, as they felt they had been lied to. And the marketing stunt opened a Pandora's box of an endless stream of heroes who seemingly died, only to return quickly. Today, it's hard not to find a hero who hasn't experienced some type of death and resurrection experience, to which we fans roll our collective eyes. The consensus of fanboys across comic book shops everywhere was essentially that Superman's death didn't kill Superman so much as it killed the concept of death. Before that, death in the comic realm was, with few exceptions, inviolable. After that, there was free license to appear to kill and bring back to life an endless line of heroes. Now nearly all heroes routinely return from the grave as we exist in this perpetual state of heroes never dying and always resurrecting. There is always some way to explain away and avoid actual physical death and physical resurrection.

The finite nature of humanity is a grim reality; heroes stay in that realm on their quests.

A true physical death, followed by a true physical bodily resurrection, could not believably happen. Alas, the Lamb of God was slain. Mortality left its nasty mark, even on the Son of God. Jesus died. Game over, save one major detail.

HE IS RISEN

Jesus rose from the dead! Truly. The claim of Jesus' physical, bodily resurrection from the dead is a stumbling block statement if ever there was one:

> "Death is swallowed up in victory." "O death, where is your victory? O death, where is your sting?" The sting of death is sin, and the power of sin is the law. But thanks be to God, who gives us the victory through our Lord Jesus Christ.
> (1 CORINTHIANS 15:54–57)

The unbelieving world cries foul. Faith in the resurrection of Christ Jesus is said to be impossible to believe. Arguments against Jesus' resurrection from the dead suggest Christians invent traditions over truth, fiction instead of fact, and emphasize mythology rather than miracles. The intended conclusion is that the resurrection of Christ couldn't have scientifically occurred; therefore, Jesus is a legend, not a Lord.

Christ's resurrection from the dead is a true miracle. It should not be so readily dismissed as mythology. Though for argument's sake, let us keep in mind that much fact can be found in different folklores. The dragon legends undoubtedly came from humankind's ancient encounters with dinosaurs. The kraken was most likely a giant sea squid that once foundered a primitive fishing boat and grew in size in its retelling as one of early humanity's big-fish stories. The unicorn was first described by fifth century BC Greek historian Ctesias, who likely observed an Indian rhinoceros. He wrote that it was as large as a horse, had a white body, purple head, and blue eyes. It had a cubit-long horn on its forehead that was red at the tip, black in the middle, and white at the base.[41] Layers of embellished fantasy have been added over time, but they were laid upon original truths. And what of the peculiar story of resurrection from the dead of the phoenix, rising to new life from its own ashes?

THE PHOENIX

The phoenix is a uniquely rare and ancient resurrection story. It is widely known throughout the world from Western culture to the Far East, and yet its origin is hazy when examined through the annals of time. Hesiod is the oldest from classical antiquity to make mention of the phoenix in seventh century BC, but Herodotus's writing, in the fifth century BC, leads history sleuths to Egypt. Herodotus writes:

> They [the Egyptians] have also another sacred bird called the phoenix which I myself have never seen, except in pictures. Indeed it is a great rarity, even in Egypt, only coming there (according to the accounts of the people of Heliopolis) once in five hundred years, when the old phoenix dies. Its size and appearance, if it is like the pictures, are

---

41   Ctesias, *La Perse / L'Inde*, trans. René Henry (Brussels: Office de Publicité, 1947), 80–82.

as follow:—The plumage is partly red, partly golden, while the general make and size are almost exactly that of the eagle. They tell a story of what this bird does, which does not seem to me to be credible: that he comes all the way from Arabia [Phoenicia], and brings the parent bird, all plastered over with myrrh, to the temple of the Sun, and there buries the body. In order to bring him, they say, he first forms a ball of myrrh as big as he finds that he can carry; then he hollows out the ball and puts his parent inside, after which he covers over the opening with fresh myrrh, and the ball is then of exactly the same weight as at first; so he brings it to Egypt, plastered over as I have said, and deposits it in the temple of the Sun. Such is the story they tell of the doings of this bird.[42]

The Egyptians venerated the bird and celebrated it in association with their worship of the sun god Ra. Variant stories of the dying phoenix's flight to Heliopolis included it sacrificing itself in the altar fire, from which the young new phoenix then rose. The sacrifice, rising rebirth from the dead, and eternal renewing essence of the phoenix has been perpetuated and elaborated in writing ever since. The Romans associated the bird with their eternal city, even going so far as to mint coins with a phoenix on one side.

Many of the Early Church Fathers connected the phoenix to Christ's resurrection from the dead. Clement of Rome, who lived in the generation after Peter, wrote an epistle to the Corinthians, who were struggling with belief in the resurrection of Christ. Clement built up his argument by the observance of resurrection in nature: the death of winter springs to new life; seeds shoot up and bear fruit; night gives way to the dawn. Clement then referenced the phoenix, suggesting both the natural world and the secular world reinforce resurrection imagery. Hence, it should not be too difficult to believe Christ rose from the dead.[43]

---

42   Herodotus, *The Histories of Herodotus* (1858 translation), trans. George Rawlinson (Pontiac, MI: Scribe Publishing, 2018), book II.

43   Philip Schaff, *Ante-Nicene Christianity, A.D. 100–325*, History of the Christian Church, vol. 2 (Grand Rapids, MI: Christian Classics Ethereal Library, n.d.), 572, https://ccel.org/ccel/s/schaff/hcc2/cache/hcc2.pdf.

Church Fathers Cyril of Jerusalem, Tertullian, Origen, Ambrose, and Jerome all incorporated the phoenix as allegory within their teachings of Christian doctrine on Christ's resurrection.[44] Details continued to be emphasized through the ages. The phoenix's association with the palm tree[45] also drew attention from the Church. Burnt palm ashes from the prior year's Palm Sunday are used to mark believers at the beginning of Lent, culminating with the celebration of Christ's resurrection from the grave on Easter morning. The phoenix story has endured through popular literature; Dante's *Inferno,* John Milton's *Paradise Lost,* and Shakespeare's *Henry VIII* all give the phoenix a referencing nod. Even *Harry Potter* has repopularized a version of the phoenix for our current generation.

Cynics will continue to scoff, asserting that the legend of the phoenix far predates the resurrection of Jesus. Yet intriguingly, once again it is quite plausible that the original seeds of truth about the phoenix are actually from the ancient Hebrew oral tradition of creation as well as Old Testament prophecies of the resurrection of the dead foreshadowing Christ. Where did the phoenix mythology come from? The mystic bird's sun-fire creational association came from the Egyptians, and the regeneration-resurrection aspect was most likely applied later by the Greeks.

The origin of the phoenix mythology appears to come in the story of the *benu,* an Egyptian sun god in the form of a bird, which was understood to have ascended out of the chaos-waters at creation. This bird was closely associated with the creator sun god and believed to be the soul of Ra.[46] Ra, believed to be an eternal deity, is customarily depicted in Egyptian hieroglyphics as a man with the head of a bird, often with a sun disk resting above him.

Let us recall the post-tower-of-Babel telephone game through the godless generations. Various people groups roamed the earth. They were

---

44   See for example *Cyril of Jerusalem, Gregory Nazianzen,* Nicene and Post-Nicene Fathers, Series II, vol. 7, ed. Philip Schaff (Grand Rapids, MI: Christian Classics Ethereal Library, n.d.), Lecture XVIII, https://ccel.org/ccel/s/schaff/npnf207/cache/npnf207.pdf.

45   In *Metamorphoses,* Ovid wrote that the phoenix built its nest in "some swaying palm" before departing to "Hyperion's temple" (345).

46   David Fideler, *Jesus Christ, Sun of God: Ancient Cosmology and Early Christian Symbolism* (Wheaton, IL: Quest Books, 1993), 248–49.

separated by language in a culture long devoid of faith, yet faintly familiar with Yahweh's origin of the world.[47] The early Egyptians, distant descendants of Noah's son Ham, would have known the oral traditions of a Spirit hovering over the waters at creation (Genesis 1:2), of a promised son of God (Genesis 3:15), and of another bird once again hovering over the chaos-waters after the flood and the rebirth of the world (Genesis 8:6–11). Is it so hard to conceive of an ancient godless people, who had some knowledge of true creation, centuries later coming up with a creational explanation of a one-of-a-kind bird that hovered over chaos-waters and served as the soul of their sun god? Perhaps the significance of the Genesis account is worth noting in the foreshadowing of another bird, one that descended from the heavens and hovered over the baptismal waters of Jesus in the Jordan River.

Where does the resurrection of the dead concept come from? The Greeks, ever mindful of asserting their Hellenizing dominance on other cultures, built upon the phoenix myth. They soon associated the phoenix with the Greek sun god, Apollo, further enhanced its fiery characteristics, and wove it into the deeper fabric of their other fables. More importantly, the Greeks had access to much historic literature, including Old Testament evidence of a belief in a resurrection from the dead.

RESURRECTION

Before Jesus was raised from the dead, God spoke through His prophets and told the world what was to happen. Several testifying Scripture references follow: "For I know that my Redeemer lives, and at the last He will stand upon the earth" (Job 19:25). "Your dead shall live; their bodies shall rise. You who dwell in the dust, awake and sing for joy! For your dew is a dew of light, and the earth will give birth to the dead" (Isaiah 26:19). "But at that time your people shall be delivered, everyone whose name

47   The ancient Athenian philosopher Plato once referenced a golden age before the Greeks, when humankind shared the same language. In classic Greco-deity punishing style, it was believed the gods intervened and confused their speech. See John McClintock and James Strong, *Cyclopedia of Biblical, Theological, and Ecclesiastical Literature*, vol. 1 (Grand Rapids, MI: Baker Publishing Group, 1968), 590.

shall be found written in the book. And many of those who sleep in the dust of the earth shall awake, some to everlasting life, and some to shame and everlasting contempt" (Daniel 12:1–2). "For You will not abandon my soul to Sheol, or let Your holy one see corruption" (Psalm 16:10).

Hesiod, the oldest Greek mythology author, wrote between 750–650 BC and published roughly around 700 BC. Moses, Job, David's psalms, Elijah, Jonah, and Isaiah all predate him, as do their writings. Not only was there ample testimony on record of the resurrection of the dead, but there was also faith in God to do it. The source of the resurrection of the dead came from the one true God, Yahweh. The tantalizing lure of eternal life and immortality would have been irresistibly easy to incorporate into stories forever after.

The apocryphal book of 2 Maccabees, written in second century BC, also attested to a hope of a resurrection of the dead. One story relates how seven brothers, while being put to death for their faith, stated, "You accursed wretch, you dismiss us from this present life, but the King of the universe will raise us up to an everlasting renewal of life, because we have died for His laws" (2 Maccabees 7:9 RSV).

The Jewish people in first century AD still hoped and demonstrated faith in the resurrection of the dead. On one occasion, Jesus consoled Martha, the distraught sister of Lazarus, who had died days earlier.

> Jesus said to her, "Your brother will rise again." Martha said to Him, "I know that he will rise again in the resurrection on the last day." Jesus said to her, "I am the resurrection and the life. Whoever believes in Me, though he die, yet shall he live, and everyone who lives and believes in Me shall never die."
>
> (JOHN 11:23–26)

Martha's testimony affirms the hope in the resurrection to come, though Jesus also blessed her by bringing her brother back to life that very day.

And finally, one Sunday, it happened. In the early dawn hour, some of the women in Jesus' company hastened to His tomb. They wanted to anoint His dead body with perfumes and spices, as was the custom.

They were in for a shocking surprise. The women were greeted by an angel come from heaven:

> But the angel said to the women, "Do not be afraid, for I know that you seek Jesus who was crucified. He is not here, for He has risen, as He said. Come, see the place where He lay. Then go quickly and tell His disciples that He has risen from the dead, and behold, He is going before you to Galilee; there you will see Him. See, I have told you." So they departed quickly from the tomb with fear and great joy, and ran to tell His disciples. And behold, Jesus met them and said, "Greetings!" And they came up and took hold of His feet and worshiped Him. Then Jesus said to them, "Do not be afraid; go and tell My brothers to go to Galilee, and there they will see Me." (MATTHEW 28:5–10)

Go and tell they did. The storytelling of Jesus rising from the grave has not ceased. The entirety of Scripture revolves around this central confession. Jesus, the Hero of heroes, came back to life. The Author of Life could not be kept down in death. Attempts to emulate Christ's resurrection have continued in literature ever since, mere literary shadow play compared to Jesus' physical resurrection from the dead. Finding a modern hero without a death-and-resurrection motif incorporated into the story would be almost as rare as sighting an actual phoenix.

Jesus, our one-of-a-kind Lord, rose on Easter morning like a phoenix from the ashes of death. The phoenix legend perhaps glows with an ancient ember of truth, a flicker of biblical prophecy of the true resurrection fulfilled by none other than Jesus. However, this resurrection was not by a sun god but by the Son of God. Some Christian institutions still utilize the phoenix as a mascot to this day. Christ's resurrection from the dead is the preeminent truth statement in all of Christendom. This Good News changed the world forever. Jesus is not dead; He is risen, and He brought back so much more with Him in His victory. Jesus' death didn't kill Jesus permanently; He rose! Therefore, Jesus' death killed death. He is "the firstborn from the dead" (Colossians 1:18).

I know that my Redeemer lives;
What comfort this sweet sentence gives!
He lives, He lives, who once was dead;
He lives, my ever-living head.[48]

---

48   "I Know That My Redeemer Lives," *LSB* 461:1.

A HOMECOMING GIFT

I am ascending to My Father and your Father, to My God and your God.

—JOHN 20:17

How a sweet and ordinary farm girl ever got into so much trouble is a marvel. Immediately following the start of her runaway adventure, she met a mentor who gave her aid. Then she made fast enemies with a rival foe. Three loyal allies soon joined her journey on a yellow-bricked road of trials. They faced their fears, vanquished the villain, and completed the quest. Yet all Dorothy wanted, ever since she'd opened her black-and-white threshold door into the bright Technicolor Land of Oz, was to go back to Kansas. Her homebound hope died when the wizard's hot-air balloon floated away without her, but a newly revealed truth quickly resurrected her faith. Dorothy learned the hard way that being home with her loved ones was her true heart's desire. A triplet of heel clicks from her magic ruby slippers was all that was needed to send her and Toto back to Kansas. She soon ascended from her enchanting slumber and found all the faces she'd so desperately missed. She was not empty-handed; she had a newfound understanding. Dorothy brought back with her critical knowledge.

THERE'S NO PLACE LIKE HOME

The classic concluding sequence of the hero's journey is a recrossing of the original threshold. The hero, compelled to return home to the world he or she previously enjoyed, seeks to do so, for the quest is complete. There is no reason for him or her to stay in the land of adventure. Order has been restored, and all wrongs have been righted. Rejoicing, fanfare, and rest are in order. A good epic story will not leave any major details or plot holes unaddressed. After Jesus rose from the grave, He was ready to return home to the Father, but not before He tied up a few loose ends.

Not only did Jesus rise from the grave, but He also physically roamed the earth for forty more days. He prepared for His departure by making several appearances to His followers. He spoke with them, ate with them, and even let them see and touch His wounds so that they would know with certainty that His resurrection was not a hoax. The number of personal eyewitnesses of Jesus' resurrection from the dead grew quickly. Jesus revealed Himself to Mary Magdalene and the women at the tomb on Easter morning, to two disciples on the road to Emmaus, to ten of the remaining eleven disciples in an upper room, and eventually all eleven together again, including Thomas.

Jesus also appeared to seven of His disciples while they were fishing, and He prepared breakfast for them on the beach. After His ascension into heaven, Jesus revealed Himself to Paul on the road to Damascus, blinding him and converting him to the Christian faith. The apostle Paul later testified in one of his epistles that Jesus had appeared to Cephas (Peter), the disciples, to a massive group of some five hundred people, to His brother James privately, and also later to himself (1 Corinthians 15:6–8).

One major plotline during Jesus' post-resurrection appearances addressed how Jesus prepared His followers, and the future Church, for ministry without His constant physical companionship in their midst:

On the evening of that day, the first day of the week, the
doors being locked where the disciples were for fear of the
Jews, Jesus came and stood among them and said to them,
"Peace be with you." When He had said this, He showed
them His hands and His side. Then the disciples were glad
when they saw the Lord. Jesus said to them again, "Peace be
with you. As the Father has sent Me, even so I am sending
you." And when He had said this, He breathed on them and
said to them, "Receive the Holy Spirit. If you forgive the sins
of any, they are forgiven them; if you withhold forgiveness
from any, it is withheld." (JOHN 20:19–23)

Perhaps the most famous of Jesus' post-resurrection appearances
has become known as the *Great Commission,* in which He charged the
gathering with specific instructions:

Now the eleven disciples went to Galilee, to the mountain to
which Jesus had directed them. And when they saw Him they
worshiped Him, but some doubted. And Jesus came and said
to them, "All authority in heaven and on earth has been given
to Me. Go therefore and make disciples of all nations, bap-
tizing them in the name of the Father and of the Son and of
the Holy Spirit, teaching them to observe all that I have com-
manded you. And behold, I am with you always, to the end of
the age." (MATTHEW 28:16–20)

Lastly, Jesus appeared to His disciples and prepared to depart from
their presence as He ascended into heaven.

And He led them out as far as Bethany, and lifting up His
hands He blessed them. While He blessed them, He parted
from them and was carried up into heaven. And they worshiped Him and returned to Jerusalem with great joy, and
were continually in the temple blessing God. (LUKE 24:50–53)

THE ASCENSION

Jesus Christ, our divine saving Hero, completed His epic divine quest. He recrossed the threshold, returned home to the heavenly realm whence He came, and sat down on His throne in majesty. Jesus was not the same as when He first departed but was forever changed. When Christ initially took on human flesh, that act was permanent. God in Christ Jesus did not shed His skin post-ascension. He ascended to heaven in bodily form, and He remains in bodily form for all eternity. There is no biblical reason provided to believe otherwise. The divine Christ entered physical space at the incarnation, but the human-divine Jesus Christ entered divine space at the ascension.

Jesus ascended from the disciples' immediate presence, into the heavenly realms, so that His message would spread through all the world. In so doing, His comprehensible local presence magnified into an incomprehensible spiritual omnipresence for all believers. If Jesus had stayed on earth post-resurrection, He would have undoubtedly become a celebrity phenomenon for gawkers. Pressure for more miracles and demands for signs would invariably come. Jesus knew the ascent of His local bodily presence away from His believers would mean an increasing of His spiritual presence for them in ways they could not imagine. The Good News message of His story would multiply. By the power of the Holy Spirit, He can be in the hearts of believers anywhere and everywhere. "For where two or three are gathered in My name, there am I among them" (Matthew 18:20). Because of His ascension, Jesus is really and truly present in, with, and under the bread and wine of Holy Communion, as the words "This is My body, this is My blood" are invoked.

Jesus ascended into heaven effectively as Master of two worlds. He came down from heaven, lived the perfect life in accordance with the Law, fulfilled the prophecies, finished His journey of redemption for all the world, and returned home to heaven. He is the noble heroic King who rules and reigns over two kingdoms, exalted over heaven and earth. Moreover, Jesus gave His subjects instructions. The evangelist Luke also wrote the Book of Acts, which immediately picks up where his Gospel ends. Luke provided a bit more of what Jesus shared with His disciples just before He ascended, up, up, and away.

> So when they had come together, they asked Him, "Lord, will You at this time restore the kingdom to Israel?" He said to them, "It is not for you to know times or seasons that the Father has fixed by His own authority. But you will receive power when the Holy Spirit has come upon you, and you will be My witnesses in Jerusalem and in all Judea and Samaria, and to the end of the earth." And when He had said these things, as they were looking on, He was lifted up, and a cloud took Him out of their sight. And while they were gazing into heaven as He went, behold, two men stood by them in white robes, and said, "Men of Galilee, why do you stand looking into heaven? This Jesus, who was taken up from you into heaven, will come in the same way as you saw Him go into heaven." (ACTS 1:6–11)

Jesus taught the apostles about what His active reign would look like moving forward. Believers today still profess their faith in His kingdom in words such as those of the Apostles' Creed. The Second Article of the Creed draws to a close, confessing Jesus' progression in His state of exaltation. Christians profess, "He descended into hell. The third day He rose again from the dead. He ascended into heaven and sits at the right hand of God the Father Almighty."

RETURN WITH THE ELIXIR

The hero has undergone a metamorphosis through the duration of his or her quest. Victory has been acquired, but the hero must bring satisfactory evidence of this triumphant accomplishment back home with him or her. An elixir of sorts is needed to provide proof of said victory. It may be a physical object or a symbolic representation of change. It may look quite different from one hero to the next: a treasure found, a relationship restored, a competition won, or a secret knowledge gained. Regardless, the hero has changed profoundly as an individual and offers inspiration to others. The hero's *return with the elixir* predictably brings remedy to earlier problems while silencing former naysayers.

Christ did not ascend empty-handed to God the Father in the heavenly realms. He returned with an elixir. What might this cure-all prize be, this treasure for which He so heroically battled? You, dear reader. You. Jesus presents us to God the Father by grace. Jesus is the sole mediator between sinful humankind and the wrath of God's judgment. Jesus' sacrifice made it so that when God the Father would look on any believer, He would only see the righteousness of Jesus, via His holy, precious bloodshed, innocent suffering, and death.

The Church, the Bride of Christ itself, is the treasure presented to His Father via His sacrifice. One of Jesus' parables mysteriously but majestically articulates this point. "The kingdom of heaven is like treasure hidden in a field, which a man found and covered up. Then in his joy he goes and sells all that he has and buys that field" (Matthew 13:44).

Our King Jesus reigns in such a way that He is the one who finds us, lost and condemned in the sinful field of the world. While He finds us, He must also let us remain covered in the sinful world as He goes to do the salvific dying, rising, and ascending. By accomplishing this, He buys the field and redeems us. Here believers and followers of Christ remain, awaiting His promised return. He will come again.

Another key component of the Christian faith is what believers confess in the Third Article of the Apostles' Creed: "I believe in . . . the resurrection of the body, and the life everlasting." This confession is not of Jesus' body resurrected toward a life everlasting—it is the body of the confessing believer. Jesus, our heroic Savior, extends His grace to all who believe, making heaven our true home too. Paul described this certainty uniquely with divine inspiration when he wrote to some of the early Christians in Philippi: "But our citizenship is in heaven, and from it we await a Savior, the Lord Jesus Christ, who will transform our lowly body to be like His glorious body, by the power that enables Him even to subject all things to Himself" (Philippians 3:20–21).

An incredible picture of the resurrection of the faithful departed comes from the Old Testament prophet Ezekiel. God gifts Ezekiel, and hearers of the text, a foreshadowing preview of the Last Day. The faithful, an army signifying the entirety of God's people, will be quickened to life again, a resurrected and glorified eternal life.

> The hand of the LORD was upon me, and He brought me out in the Spirit of the LORD and set me down in the middle of the valley; it was full of bones. And He led me around among them, and behold, there were very many on the surface of the valley, and behold, they were very dry. And He said to me, "Son of man, can these bones live?" And I answered, "O Lord GOD, You know." Then He said to me, "Prophesy over these bones, and say to them, O dry bones, hear the word of the LORD. Thus says the Lord GOD to these bones: Behold, I will cause breath to enter you, and you shall live. And I will lay sinews upon you, and will cause flesh to come upon you, and cover you with skin, and put breath in you, and you shall live, and you shall know that I am the LORD." So I prophesied as I was commanded. And as I prophesied, there was a sound, and behold, a rattling, and the bones came together, bone to its bone. And I looked, and behold, there were sinews on them, and flesh had come upon them, and skin had covered them. But there was no breath in them. Then He said to me, "Prophesy to the breath; prophesy, son of man, and say to the breath, Thus says the Lord GOD: Come from the four winds, O breath, and breathe on these slain, that they may live." So I prophesied as He commanded me, and the breath came into them, and they lived and stood on their feet, an exceedingly great army. (EZEKIEL 37:1–10)

Much like God breathed life into the dust of the earth to create Adam, the first man, so He will do so again to raise us back to life from death. He sent Christ, the Second Adam, to save humanity in this way. His Word does not return void. His promise will crescendo in truth on the

Last Day. For the dead will rise and join to be with Him forever. "Then we who are alive, who are left, will be caught up together with them in the clouds to meet the Lord in the air, and so we will always be with the Lord" (1 Thessalonians 4:17).

> Lord, let at last Thine angels come,
> To Abr'ham's bosom bear me home,
>   That I may die unfearing;
> And in its narrow chamber keep
> My body safe in peaceful sleep
>   Until Thy reappearing.
> And then from death awaken me,
> That these mine eyes with joy may see,
>   O Son of God, Thy glorious face,
>   My Savior and my fount of grace.
> Lord Jesus Christ, my prayer attend, my prayer attend,
> And I will praise Thee without end.[49]

---

49   "Lord, Thee I Love with All My Heart," *LSB* 708:3.

EPILOGUE

Occasionally, after enjoying a great epic hero story, the listener is deeply moved. It is easy for one to be so entranced in the fantasy of a great hero story that one almost dreamily fantasizes about somehow becoming part of that world with that hero. Alas, eventually, the last page of the book has been turned, the series finale culminates, or the cinema screen fades to black for the film credits to roll. The concluding experience can leave the hearer of the story profoundly moved with a somber afterglow. The story is finished. One wants to keep enjoying the hero, but the thing about finales is they're final. Quickly after the fog of emotions has passed, a buried desire bursts forth into hope. Will there perhaps be a sequel in which the hero's story will be further enjoyed?

The last line Christians confess in the Second Article of the Apostles' Creed reads, "From thence He will come to judge the living and the dead." You, dear reader of Christ's heroics, are in for an eternally delightful treat. Jesus has a promised sequel that will have no equal. Not only that, but He also invites hearers of His story to participate in the story itself, to join Him and become part of it all. His adventure is not fantasy; it is real, and He calls us to join the adventure. And the best news is that this story He invites us into is never-ending. Jesus came the first time, the first advent, when the faithful waited expectantly for the Messiah, and the Word became flesh at Christmas. He also comes into the life of the individual at Baptism. And now, together as the Church, we expectantly await His coming again, which will be a final coming, another advent.

John, the evangelist and the last living of the original twelve disciples, received an exclusive preview of this final return of the King. In extreme old age, John received a vision while exiled on the island of Patmos. This dream became known as the Book of Revelation, the last included book in the canonical Bible. The apocalyptic return of Jesus is one event, but John sees more than one vision. Like a forthcoming film with variant trailers, John sees how Jesus has overcome everything. He sees it from a heavenly context, he sees it from an earthly context, and ultimately, he sees the kingdom fully realized in the new Jerusalem.

The revelatory scenes of this advent sequel of Jesus are powerful, mind-blowing images of blockbuster proportions with no comparison: the throne of heaven, the Lamb, the opening of seals of the scroll, winged squadrons of angels, a great dragon, and the 666 mark of the beast. He sees the four horsemen of the apocalypse: war, famine, pestilence, and death. John sees the defeat of the devil as he is thrown into hell, the triumph in heaven, and the marriage banquet feast with the Lamb. He sees the Rider (Christ) on the white horse, judgment before the great white throne, a new heaven and a new earth, a new Jerusalem, and a river of life, for Jesus is most assuredly coming.

At a certain point, John sees the trial of tribulation that believers endure before they enter eternal life. It is a sight of pain and suffering. "'Who are these, clothed in white robes, and from where have they come?'... 'These are the ones coming out of the great tribulation. They have washed their robes and made them white in the blood of the Lamb'" (Revelation 7:13–14). While the depiction is of suffering and misery, that is cause for hope, for John also sees the Church Triumphant, because of Jesus.

> A great multitude that no one could number, from every nation, from all tribes and peoples and languages, standing before the throne and before the Lamb, clothed in white robes, with palm branches in their hands. (REVELATION 7:9)

A very vivid and accurate snapshot of how we will dwell in the promise of God in eternal grace, forever.

What is the Great Tribulation? It is what we are going through right now as the Church Militant. It is the very lives we live, dealing with all the difficulties and atrocities we endure as we await to join the Church Triumphant on the Last Day. The good news is that God likes to lead His people by faith through difficult seasons, and He does so ultimately in, with, and through the work of Christ. In the meantime, Jesus is preparing to make His home our home for all eternity. "In My Father's house are many rooms. If it were not so, would I have told you that I go to prepare a place for you?" (John 14:2). There is indeed no place like home.

God knows faith must clash with doubt in a sinful world while we wait for His return. He creates our faith and gives it as a gift to us. We do not have to rely on our own strength to have faith; we need only rely on His good Word to us. Consequently, as Christians, we live in a now-and-not-yet context. This true dual reality helps us understand that we are active participants in the kingdom of God, even though it will not reach its full realization until the Last Day when Christ comes back. We are in His kingdom now, but we do not yet see it in its glory. "Beloved, we are God's children now, and what we will be has not yet appeared; but we know that when He appears we shall be like Him, because we shall see Him as He is. And everyone who thus hopes in Him purifies himself as He is pure" (1 John 3:2–3).

Every week, we have an amazing gift through worship, the Divine Service. Sunday worship is not so much us serving Christ as it is Christ serving us, with mercy, grace, and forgiveness by the power of His Word. Every week we come, knowing we've been sinful, and every week the spoken Word of Christ is proclaimed over us, absolving sins. We are restored by the power of the Gospel glory story of Jesus proclaimed to us. Through the reading of the Scriptures, the preaching of the Gospel, the chanting of the psalms, the singing of the hymns, and the partaking of Holy Communion, the story of Jesus is made alive in us, chapter after chapter, episode after episode of our lives. Our epic, divine, heroic Savior, Jesus, is real, and He continues to defend us from all danger and guard and protect us from all evil.

The seeds of Christ's true narrative are evident in so much of our celebrated heroic literature, from ages past to modern triumphs. The underlying difference is that the story of Jesus actually happened. Not only is Jesus' journey true, but He also invites any and all who believe into His story and on His journey. Jesus died and paid for the sins of the world. "For God so loved the world, that He gave His only Son, that whoever believes in Him should not perish but have eternal life" (John 3:16).

Tragically, not all who hear this glory story of Jesus believe. Therefore, it is the imperative joyful obligation of Christians faithfully to continue telling the amazingly grand glory story of Christ Jesus until He returns. From generation to generation we wait, ever hopeful of His imminent nearness. Christians celebrate, worship, receive, and repeat what Christ has done for us and the world. We pray that one person more might come to faith by hearing the Good News: Jesus Christ is Lord of lords—and Lord of legends.

> On Christ's ascension I now build
>   The hope of my ascension;
> This hope alone has always stilled
>   All doubt and apprehension;
> For where the Head is, there as well
> I know His members are to dwell
>   When Christ shall come and call them.[50]

---

50   "On Christ's Ascension I Now Build," *LSB* 492:1 (© 1941 CPH).

AFTERWORD

The two young Oxford dons enjoyed an academic lawn duel as much as the next. A fair summary of their discussion might have sounded like this: "Your religion is just a myth!" C. S. Lewis barked. "No, it's a fact," J. R. R. Tolkien replied. Round and about the literary juggernauts went.

On the surface, it seemed hopelessly lost in nuance, but underneath, so much more was at stake. They weren't having a brand-new, cutting-edge debate. They were engaging in an age-old conversation that had preceded them millennia earlier and has endured another century since. Their conversation turned on just how exactly God and humankind are reconciled in relationship to each other, while making reasonable sense from the world's oldest sources of information.

Lewis, an atheist at this point in his life, loved historic mythology as well as more recent offerings such as the writings of George MacDonald.[51] He could not yet confess a faith in the God of Christianity. The ancient story of Jesus seemed too like the other myths of yore, or so his logic led him to believe. Many of the epic hero writers of antiquity had influenced him greatly. Through the collective writings of the Greeks and Romans, a pantheon of gods and heroes has built up a weighty impact on religious understanding. It has carried over to our modern generations. The ancient echo of Tolkien's discussion with Lewis can be traced to earlier examples of similar Christian apologetic debate. Justin Martyr, a second-century AD Church Father, wrote a forceful witness of Christ's supremacy over the Greek gods in his *Discourse to the Greeks*. Martyr wrote:

> Do not suppose, ye Greeks, that my separation from your customs is unreasonable and unthinking; for I found in them nothing that is holy or acceptable to God. For the very compositions of your poets are monuments of madness and intemperance. For any one who becomes the scholar of

---

51   George MacDonald was a Scottish minister and author. Many of his works, particularly *The Princess and the Goblin*, had great influence on both Lewis and Tolkien.

your most eminent instructor, is more beset by difficulties than all men besides. . . . Henceforth, ye Greeks, come and partake of incomparable wisdom, and be instructed by the Divine Word, and acquaint yourselves with the King immortal; and do not recognize those men as heroes who slaughter whole nations. For our own Ruler, the Divine Word, who even now constantly aids us, does not desire strength of body and beauty of feature, nor yet the high spirit of earth's nobility, but a pure soul, fortified by holiness, and the watchwords of our King, holy actions, for through the Word power passes into the soul. O trumpet of peace to the soul that is at war! O weapon that puttest to flight terrible passions! O instruction that quenches the innate fire of the soul! The Word exercises an influence which does not make poets: it does not equip philosophers nor skilled orators, but by its instruction it makes mortals immortal, mortals gods; and from the earth transports them to the realms above Olympus. Come, be taught; become as I am, for I, too, was as ye are. These have conquered me—the divinity of the instruction, and the power of the Word.[52]

The discourse continues to percolate in our present culture. A fascinating version of this conversation is currently playing out today in the comic book industry. Marvel Comics has enjoyed a massively successful box office run with (at the time of this writing) roughly twenty consecutive films in their Marvel Cinematic Universe (MCU). Fan interest and enthusiasm are at all-time highs. The MCU has no end in sight. However, a major thematic shake-up is happening in the source of their character's powers. Most of the Marvel heroes were created in the 1960s and reflect the nuclear-age societal fears of that time. The popular hero's origin of powers came from sources such as gamma radiation or radioactive

---

52   Justin Martyr, *Discourse to the Greeks*, chapters 1, 5. Ante-Nicene Fathers, vol. 1, ed. Philip Schaff (Grand Rapids, MI: Christian Classics Ethereal Library, n.d.), 721, 725, https://www.ccel.org/ccel/s/schaff/anf01/cache/anf01.pdf.

spider bites. The other explained source for superpowers is evolution. The further advancement of humanity on a higher level comes from genetic mutations, as in the X-Men. Both superpower sources are easily supported and explained away by an atheistic or scientific worldview.

However, other potentially massive story lines and concepts have been developed that provide alternative sources of power for these heroes. In one instance, the writers created something called the "God power." Essentially, this theory posits that every single superhero with a power possesses it only because they had some type of interaction with an ultimate being source—hence, the God power. God working through humans. If that wasn't enough, villains presumably get their superpowers from what Marvel comic writers describe as "The One Who Dwells Below." It remains to be seen in the comic world how this and other alternative story lines about where powers come from will all be reconciled, but new concepts have the potential of rocking the Marvel Universe to the core, with implications perhaps greater than they initially intended.[53]

Many of the world's treasured hero stories share more than meets the eye on a surface-level reading. After a good dusting of discernment, a clear, familiar reoccurring theme is observable. It is almost as if many of these age-old stories, and a healthy dose of modern ones, are somehow the same story. These include grand epics bearing unintended blessings with the underlying salvific rescue message they bring. These great hero's quest stories carry a glimpse of the redemption of humankind. The reason this seemingly same story is told over and over is that the underlying archetypal hero is none other than our Savior, Jesus Christ.

Christ's epic quest of redemption is woven into creation and the human experience, inescapably so. This truth, embedded in our subconscious, is often at the root of these stories. Our sinful world craves for this truth to be real and transformative. This explains why these stories draw such wide appeal across many demographics. One talented theologian and scholar phrased it this way after examining the Gospel of Mark in deep detail in comparison to Homer's epics.

---

53   Chip Zdarsky, *X-Men/Fantastic Four* #1 (New York: Marvel Worldwide, Inc., 2020).

Such parallels show the *superiority* of Jesus to Odysseus, and they can be drawn with the understanding that the Homeric epics (as well as other ancient Near Eastern myths) provided a *cultural preparation* for the true expression of the interaction between God and man, namely, that which has occurred in the person of Jesus Christ. Humanly speaking this is likely one of the reasons that the "story of Jesus" resonated throughout the Mediterranean world and in less than three centuries conquered the Roman Empire.[54]

When these classical and modern hero stories are told, reimagined, and retold again, they speak an ancient language of a greater truth about Jesus and His redeeming act of saving the world. Christ's grand adventure, when ultimately brought to light with the clear Word of God, is not merely a solo journey. Jesus invites any and all, by grace through faith, into His adventure with Him for all eternity.

Unfortunately, sin, death, and the devil do their best to stand in the way. Stalwart disbelievers and atheist doubters who despise, reject, or even mock the certainty of Jesus' heroic story have excelled at inventing their own augmented hero manifestations. The rise of the antihero in pop culture provides strong evidence of this undermining tendency. The last few generations have increasingly cast aside the heroes of yore, who were full of light, purity, and nobility, and traded them for darker heroes with gritty, earthly tones. Antiheroes lack the standard pure idealistic characteristics. They are typically rough around the edges, possess dubious desires, and blur the lines of right and wrong. They are often rebellious realists who stand up to authority. They may act in self-interest and even have criminal tendencies. They are vigilantes who push the boundaries of moralism to the extreme.

Regrettably, the concept of the antihero has become a more popular device of modern-day storytelling. It is no surprise, in a fallen world, that more people identify with a flaw-ridden character rather than a pure, noble

---

54   James Voelz, *Mark 8:27–16:20*, Concordia Commentary (St. Louis: Concordia Publishing House, 2019), 600.

hero. Many sinners, particularly those who deny Christ, can deeply relate to unscrupulous characters who make attempts at heroic acts. The inner psyche of fallen humanity prefers to see the self as hero as opposed to the one being helped, saved, or redeemed.

Joseph Campbell capitalized quite well, knowing humans fancy themselves as heroes. His storytelling technique in *The Hero's Journey* has influenced countless people in generations past his own. Campbell stumbled upon something amazing with his analysis of the hero's journey. Presumably, and perhaps lamentably, he never fully realized just how amazing it is, regarding its apparent Christological significance. He routinely spoke against Christianity in interviews throughout his career. He was dismissive of Jesus as God and viewed the resurrection of Christ more like a clown act than an act of the divine. He gravitated more toward pantheism and did not care for the moral code of orthodox Christianity.[55]

What Campbell did accomplish was to pique the fascination of the hero concept in the minds of many to follow. The concepts of not only the epic hero, but also of becoming one's own self-actualizing hero, easily played into the hands of a world in love and impressed with itself. Most likely, Campbell denied Christ for the rest of his days. It is an epic tragedy he did not have a Tolkienesque friend.

The Gospel cannot be suppressed. Devout Christian author J. R. R. Tolkien turned the hero's journey on its head. His beloved literary character Bilbo the hobbit is not the traditional self-actualizing hero, but quite the contrary. Bilbo is the fumbling, bumbling non-heroic figure, routinely being rescued by Gandalf, the Christ figure. Tolkien's books of Middle Earth invite readers to discover being rescued on the journey. This type of literary hero influence is ever so powerful, with eternal implications. One of Tolkien's most profound acts was proclaiming the Gospel to his friend and author C. S. Lewis, and the Spirit used that witness to cross Lewis over from atheism to faith in Christ.

Doctrines written by humankind were a stumbling block to Lewis. How were they any different than other ancient writing? Tolkien showed

---

55   Bill Moyers, *Joseph Campbell and the Power of Myth*, PBS series, 1988.

Lewis[56] that doctrines are not the primary source of Christianity. Instead, history is specifically the history of Jesus. God teaches through story, history—His story. Doctrines are essentially translations (confessions) of what God has already expressed in His own language in Scripture. That more adequate language of God's was the actual incarnation, crucifixion, and resurrection of Christ. When Lewis began to see that the primary language of Christianity is not humanly written doctrines but the historically lived language of Jesus' birth, death, and resurrection, it began to transform him as only the Gospel can. Once the gift of faith is received, the veil is lifted. The aspects of the transcendent story of Jesus can be found in many of the stories of the past and can inspire authors to write new ones.

By the power of the Spirit working through God's Word, Clive Staples Lewis finally had his divine epiphany. He began to see that Christianity did not have to be interfaced with primarily as a doctrinal system of beliefs. Rather, one can first approach it as a sequence of historical events (which it is) and then allow the doctrinal landscape to fill in around it. Thus, Lewis could embrace the Christian faith with hope as the one true myth, whereas pagan myths were hopelessly humankind's myths. Lewis became delighted to discover that the Christian faith's enchanting qualities were in fact born of the real world and not from imagination.

If Lewis had to pinpoint a determining factor in his ultimate shift to Christianity, it was the concept of divine Sonship. That concept shone through George MacDonald's writings and inspired Lewis and others all the more. Christ's death and resurrection redeems and makes people adopted sons and daughters, brought into His royal divine family. "He has granted to us His precious and very great promises, so that through them you may become partakers of the divine nature, having escaped from the corruption that is in the world because of sinful desire" (2 Peter 1:4). For Lewis, the ability to share in Christ's divine nature made Christianity stand out from everything else. To be made an inheritor of Jesus' kingdom

---

56   C.S. Lewis's letter, October 18, 1931, in Alistair McGrath, *C. S. Lewis—A Life: Eccentric Genius, Reluctant Prophet* (Carol Stream, IL: Tyndale House Publishers, Inc., 2013).

meant everything. Not only was C. S. Lewis brought to faith by the Spirit, but he also became one of the premiere apologists of Christianity in the last century, through his lectures, theology books, and certainly his *Chronicles of Narnia* children's fantasy books.

Jesus said, "Truly, I say to you, unless you turn and become like children, you will never enter the kingdom of heaven" (Matthew 18:3). This is just as true for a young child as it is for the approach of the adult. A humble, childlike spirit is critical for seeking and learning the faith, as well as the invariable conversations that arise.

The God-man reconciliation conversation has continued into my own home. My youngest son, the laughing fox of a boy he is, once approached me with a playful yet serious question. "Dad, are Superman and Batman real?" He was four at the time. "Well," I said, "they're real characters, but not actually people in real life." My son was processing this new mind-blowing information when I said, "We want them to be real, though, don't we?" He grinned and nodded his head, "Yeah!" "Why?" I asked. He thought for a second. "So they can save us." "Right," I said. "But who *actually* saves us?" "Jesus!" he said, smiling. "That's right, son; that's right."

> Like a mighty army
> 　Moves the Church of God;
> Brothers, we are treading
> 　Where the saints have trod.
> We are not divided,
> 　All one body we,
> One in hope and doctrine,
> 　One in charity.
> Onward, Christian soldiers,
> 　Marching as to war,
> With the cross of Jesus
> 　Going on before.[57]

57　"Onward, Christian Soldiers," *LSB* 662:2.

ACKNOWLEDGEMENTS

would like to offer many thanks to the outstanding ensemble team at Concordia Publishing House. Their hard work, dedication, and commitment to their craft makes them a Justice League of literary giants. I also share special gratitude to Wayne Palmer, my editorial Alfred in the Batcave on this project.

Much appreciation to Rev. Dr. Paul Maier, for always picking up the phone and granting prompt replies with Jedi-like wisdom and skill. I am also particularly grateful for the assemblage of endorsers of this book. Your words are gracious and much appreciated.

I am indebted to the dear saints of Bethel Lutheran Raglan, a warm shire of a congregation within which to serve and work. Specifically, I'd like to thank Jeannie Hughes and James Gray, my right and left arms in the ministry respectively. Jeannie, our Wonder Woman in the office with a memory bank more impressive than Google, and James, a trusty Samwise Gamgee if ever there was one.

To Kara, my wife, best friend, and best proofreader—you are the consummate Groovelicious Marvelizer. To my father, David, a source of constant encouragement, who cared enough to drive the teen version of myself and a carload of my friends to the Chicago Comic Con on more than one occasion. Special thanks to Magistra's "Little Latin Library of Classical Antiquity" for long checkouts and no overdue fines. I would be remiss if I did not include my dachshund, Doppelbock—my lone morning companion, always willing to wake up in the early predawn hours with me for manuscript writing.

And a reverent tip of the cap to Christ, who gives me strength.

Alighieri, Dante. *The Divine Comedy of Dante Alighieri: Hell, Purgatory, Paradise*. The Harvard Classics. Vol. 20. Translated by Henry F. Cary. Edited by Charles W. Eliot. New York: P. F. Collier and Son, 1909.

Bourne, Ella. "The Messianic Prophecy in Vergil's Fourth Eclogue." *The Classical Journal*, vol. 11, no. 7 (April 1916): 390–400.

Campbell, Joseph. *The Hero with A Thousand Faces*. 3rd ed. Novato, CA: New World Library, 2008.

Carpenter, Humphrey. *J. R. R. Tolkien: A Biography*. Boston, MA: Houghton Mifflin Company, 2000.

Chemnitz, Martin. *The Two Natures in Christ*. Translated by J. A. O. Preus. St. Louis, MO: Concordia Publishing House, 1971.

Commission on Worship of the LCMS. *Lutheran Service Book*. St. Louis, MO: Concordia Publishing House, 2006.

Ctesias. *La Perse / L'Inde*. Translated by René Henry. Brussels: Office de Publicité, 1947.

Cyril of Jerusalem, Gregory Nazianzen. Nicene and Post-Nicene Fathers. Series II. Vol. 7. Edited by Philip Schaff. Grand Rapids, MI: Christian Classics Ethereal Library, n.d. https://ccel.org/ccel/s/schaff/npnf207/cache/npnf207.pdf.

Fideler, David. *Jesus Christ, Sun of God: Ancient Cosmology and Early Christian Symbolism*. Wheaton, IL: Quest Books, 1993.

Gibbs, Jeffrey A. *Matthew 1:1–11:1*. Concordia Commentary. St. Louis, MO: Concordia Publishing House, 2006.

———. *Matthew 11:2–20:34*. Concordia Commentary. St. Louis, MO: Concordia Publishing House, 2010.

Herodotus. *The Histories of Herodotus*. Translation by George Rawlinson (1858). Pontiac, MI: Scribe Publishing, 2018.

Herzberg, Max J. *Myths and Their Meaning*. Boston, MA: Allyn and Bacon, Inc., 1984.

Just, Arthur A. *Luke 1:1–9:50*. Concordia Commentary. St. Louis, MO: Concordia Publishing House, 1997.

———. *Luke 9:51–24:53*. Concordia Commentary. St. Louis, MO: Concordia Publishing House, 1997.

Kitzhaber, Albert R., and Stoddard Malarkey. *Myths, Fables, and Folktales*. New York, NY: Holt, Reinhart and Winston, 1974.

Kottmeyer, William. *The Trojan War*. Great Britain: Webster Publishing Company, 1952.

Lewis, C. S. *The Lion, the Witch and the Wardrobe*. New York: Harper Collins, 1950.

Luther, Martin. *Luther's Small Catechism with Explanation*. St. Louis: Concordia Publishing House, 2017.

Maier, Paul L. *In the Fullness of Time: A Historian Looks at Christmas, Easter, and the Early Church*. San Francisco: Harper San Francisco, 1991.

———. *Josephus: The Essential Writings*. Grand Rapids, MI: Kregel Publications, 1988.

Martyr, Justin. *Discourse to the Greeks*. Ante-Nicene Fathers. Vol. 1. Edited by Philip Schaff. Grand Rapids, MI: Christian Classics Ethereal Library, n.d. https://www.ccel.org/ccel/s/schaff/anf01/cache/anf01.pdf.

McClintock, John, and James Strong. *Cyclopedia of Biblical, Theological, and Ecclesiastical Literature*. Vol. 1. Grand Rapids, MI: Baker Publishing Group, 1968.

McGrath, Alister. *C. S. Lewis—A Life: Eccentric Genius, Reluctant Prophet*. Carol Stream, IL: Tyndale House Publishers, Inc., 2013.

Morden, Daniel, and Hugh Lupton. *War with Troy: The Story of Achilles*. 2nd ed. Cambridge, UK: Cambridge School Classics Project, 2003.

Morford, Mark P. O., and Robert J. Lenardon. *Classical Mythology*. 4th ed. New York, NY: Longman, 1991.

Moyers, Bill. *Joseph Campbell and the Power of Myth*. PBS series, 1988.

Ovid. *The Metamorphoses of Ovid*. Translated by Mary M. Innes. London, England: Penguin Books, 1955.

Pink, Arthur W. *Exposition of the Gospel of John*. Swengel, PA: Bible Truth Depot, 1923.

Raglan, Lord. *The Hero: A Study in Tradition, Myth and Drama*. Reprint edition. Mineola, NY: Dover Publications, 2011.

Schaff, Philip. *Ante-Nicene Christianity, A.D. 100–325*. History of the Christian Church. Vol. 2. Grand Rapids, MI: Christian Classics Ethereal Library, n.d. https://ccel.org/ccel/s/schaff/hcc2/cache/hcc2.pdf.

Scharlemann, Martin H. "'He Descended into Hell': An Interpretation of 1 Peter 3:18–20." *Concordia Theological Monthly*, vol. 27, no. 2 (February 1956): 81–94.

Seltz, Martin A., and Frank Stoldt. *With One Voice*. Minneapolis, MN: Augsburg Fortress, 1995.

Virgil. *Great Books of the Western World: Virgil*. Edited by Robert Maynard Hutchins. Chicago, IL: William Benton Publisher, Encyclopedia Britannica, Inc., 1952.

Voelz, James. *Mark 8:27–16:20*. Concordia Commentary. St. Louis, MO: Concordia Publishing House, 2019.

Vogler, Christopher. *The Writer's Journey: Mythic Structure for Writers*. 3rd ed. Studio City, CA: Michael Wiese Productions, 2007.

Zdarsky, Chip. *X-Men/Fantastic Four* #1. New York: Marvel Worldwide, Inc., 2020.